VAASTU

THE INDIAN ART OF PLACEMENT

design and decorate

homes to reflect

eternal spiritual

principles

ROHIT ARYA

Destiny Books
Rochester, Vermont

D0089443

Destiny Books
One Park Street
Rochester, Vermont 05767
www.InnerTraditions.com

Destiny Books is a division of Inner Traditions International

LIBRARY OF CONGRESS CATALOGING-IN-PUBLICATION DATA
Arya, Rohit.
Vaastu : the Indian art of placement : design and decorate homes to reflect
eternal spiritual principles / Rohit Arya.
        p. cm.
ISBN 0-89281-885-9 (alk. paper)
1. Architecture, Hindu—India. 2. Vaastu—India. I. Title.
NA1501 .A885 2000
133.3'33—dc21
00-060304

Printed and bound in the United States of America

10   9   8   7   6   5   4   3   2   1

Text design and layout by Virginia L. Scott Bowman
This book was typeset in Life with Felix Titling as the display typeface

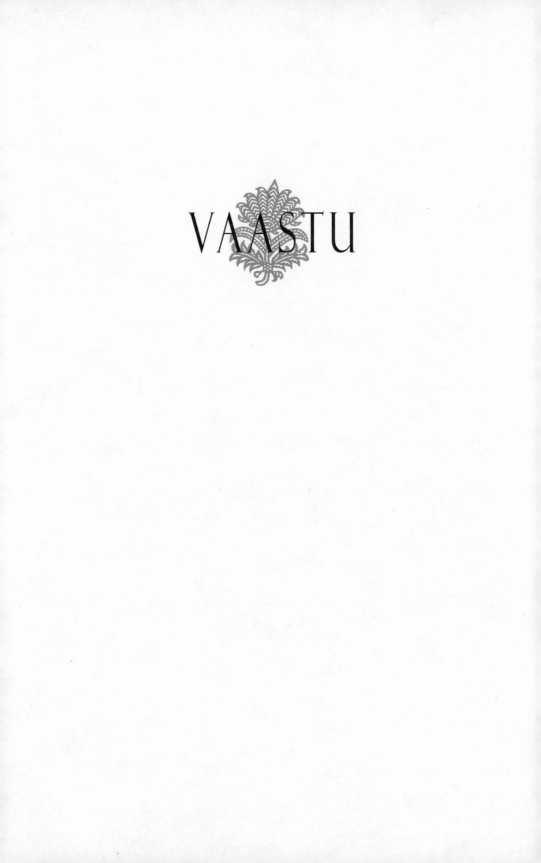

VAASTU

CONTENTS

INTRODUCTION

Architecture is one of humankind's greatest means for celebrating our place in the natural world. It is a conscious, rational effort to create harmony. The spirit of the world is acknowledged, even as structures are reared to make it more manageable. Architecture is also a phenomenon of urban life. The country house was too close to nature to attempt to order it, but the city or town uses architecture as an act of self-assertion in the face of nature's harsh realities.

India can lay claim to the oldest urban settlements ever known to humankind—the towns of the Harappan plains, circa 3000 B.C. It also had a culture that adored and exalted nature yet used one word—*nagarika*—to describe both the city dweller and the cultured human being. Architecture in India therefore had very strong urban moorings from its inception.

Fortunately, Indian culture has always valued the transcendent cosmic aspects of art. Hence the striking distinctiveness, the idiosyncratic originality, of *vaastu shastra,* the Indian art of placement. Vaastu shastra reaches out to the universe even as it simultaneously imposes structure upon it. It is a strange amalgam of science and religion, of design and instinct—perhaps inevitable for a practice that has lasted over two millennia and has only now been taken off the list of endangered arts. Vaastu concerns itself with the subtle complexities of the energy system that is a human being in relationship to both the natural and designed environments. Its links with geomancy are especially strong, and its fundamental philosophy is in agreement with feng shui, even though both differ widely in details. To state it simply, vaastu is the creation of forms that are in harmony with the natural laws of the cosmos.

At its most practical, vaastu lays down certain principles that orient and plan each element of a building from the big-picture considerations such as shape and size to the details of where windows and doors should be placed. In traditional India, building a house was not just an investment for the future. It was also a religious act, one of the vows made by the groom to the bride. She accepted him on the condition that he build an edifice for the public good: a wayside shelter, a temple, or an inn. The private and public spheres of a person's life were never considered to be separate compartments. The individual expression of self, manifest in building a house, was always to be tempered by the deference to traditional wisdom and its principles. Such balance was believed to bring about prosperity and the contentment of an enriched public life. For, as defined in the Rig Veda, vaastu is derived from the phrase *vasanti praminae yatra,* "a place where living beings reside." To make such a place a representative of the cosmos was therefore an attempt to live life more fully.

This book seeks to keep alive the spirit of vaastu. Wisdom is not restricted by history, time, or culture. The moment is now for vaastu to take its place on the honor roll of ancient arts of the world, and become accessible to all.

1
THE HISTORY OF VAASTU

The great gods in Hinduism form a triad—Brahma the Creator, Vishnu the Preserver, and Shiva, He Who Dissolves Creation. In popular mythology these three great gods are prone to errors of action; their superabundant energies cause them to act before considering the results that may follow.

One such mistake was committed by Brahma—ever prone to such mishaps—because he couldn't resist experimenting with creation. Out of the void Brahma created a humanoid form so monstrous that, on the humanoid's day of birth, his shadow fell across the earth like a second night. When this giant began to expand at an alarming rate, Brahma was pleased; his powers of creation had lost none of their vibrancy. But to the universe at large, this ever expanding creature was a source of terror, for he was hungry. He bellowed across the wastes of space that he would satisfy his hunger with anything in his path.

The lesser gods complained bitterly to Brahma. "Why must we bear the consequences of your creative fits? This creature will devour us first, you later, and all of creation in the end. Do something!"

Brahma, suddenly sobered by these plaints, realized his responsibilities to the other progeny of his creation. He assembled a task force of the *asthadigapalakas,* the guardians of the eight cardinal directions. Together they snuck up behind the monster and, in an unchivalrous but effective move, hurled themselves onto him in a cosmic tackle, squashing him flat onto the earth. Brahma added his considerable weight to the center, and literally ground the monster down into the soil. Eventually forty-five gods were employed to sit on the monster and keep him in place; their positions can be seen on the classic grid used by Indians to decipher the vaastu of any site (figure 1).

Now it was the monster's turn to complain. "Why do you gods punish me for behaving according to my nature, a nature Brahma gave me to begin with? Is this fair? And by the way, I am still hungry!"

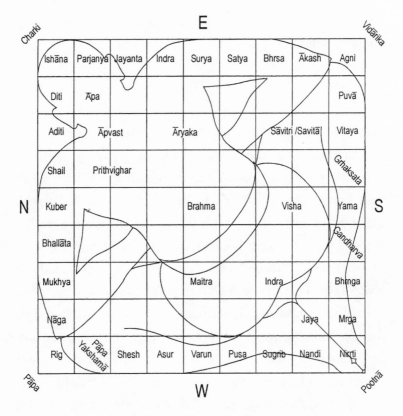

Figure 1. The vaastu grid.

Brahma felt the humanoid's arguments had merit, so the great god worked out a compromise. The demon would become immortal, provided he did not budge from his place on the earth. And in the future any person who built a structure of any kind could do so only after worshiping the demon, newly named Vaastu Purusha. Those who followed this order would be blessed; they who did not would risk the demon's wrath. This story would ever be fresh, reminding people of their obligation to feed the hunger of Vaastu Purusha, who now became part of the earth itself.

Myths always conceal some eternal principle. We can see Vaastu Purusha as the conscious life energy of the earth. It is a male principle, the yang to the yin of the Mother Goddess Earth. The actual life force of Earth is called *vastu*, while the manifestation of this force in all objects that reside within or on the earth is called *vaastu*. *Vas* means "to live" or, even better, "to be." Many attempts have been made to link Vaastu Purusha to the eternal Purusha, the Primordial Man of the Vedas and Upanishads, who sacrificed himself so that the universe might come into being. Thus, by worshiping Vaastu Purusha one develops the conscious, aware, and joyous attitude to life that is the foundation of vaastu.

As Shilpa Ratnam says, "Vaastu is the energy of life. Vaastu is the ummanifest. Vaastu is the matter of all matter. Vaastu is the microcosmos, it is the macrocosmos. Vaastu Purusha is the spark of the soul within."

And yet deeper still, at a subterranean level, operates another mythical belief. Many ancient cultures have viewed man as the reflection of all creation—man as a microcosmos to the macrocosmos without. That ideal worked in the temples of Egypt, Greece, and India. Indeed, in India every well-designed Hindu temple is a Cosmic Man.

But simultaneously every temple, and by association

every human, takes on the proportions of the *Yupa Stambha*—the cosmic pillar, the Axis Mundi or center of the universe. Every structure built, but especially a temple, is thus a re-creation of that Yupa Stambha, a creative cycle of alignment with the cosmos that is ever fresh, for each person has to make the commitment anew. This is one of the reasons for the promise made in the marriage ceremony to build a public structure. It was an acknowledgment of the special place man held in the cosmos and of his gratitude for that. Every human, male or female, was a personification of the center, the Axis Mundi. A house or temple or rest house was built to provide external evidence of this profound realization.

The most compelling evidence of the pre-Vedic roots of vaastu is to be found in the archaeological remains of Harappa, a civilization of the Indus Valley. Harappan culture was imbued with vaastu principles. Sites of their ancient urban clusters dot the northwestern contours of the Indian peninsula, extending as far as Afghanistan in the north and deep into the hinterland of Gujarat in the south. The Harappan people had a script, indecipherable even to computer simulations of today, and eerily similar to the runelike hieroglyphics found on Easter Island in the Pacific, quite literally half a world away. The Harappans had a religion, which seems to both predate and confirm the Vedic-Yogic traditions of later India. On one of their square seals used in trading, or perhaps for currency, sits a Vedic Pashupati (Shiva, lord of the animals) in a yogic posture of *udharvalinga*. This is at least 1,500 years too early, according to religious scholars' established timeline.

Above all, these cities of the plain were urban. A density of 30,000 to 100,000 inhabitants per square mile was common. And every feature of these cities, especially the older sites, conforms to vaastu tenets in a manner that staggers the imagination. The streets were built to plan and the points of the compass were the guides (figure 2). In some towns the streets were so perfectly aligned with the elements that the wind acted as a natural garbage collector, wafting debris along to convenient loops in the corners, where they

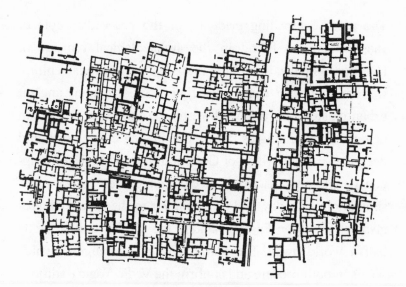

Figure 2. A Harappan city.

could be collected later. The streets were up to thirty feet wide, straight as an arrow and crossing at right angles in accordance with the vaastu tenet of using the square as the basic unit of construction. Living quarters were usually concentrated in one part of town, a rectangular cluster set apart from the citadels rising over the cities. The hot winds dictated that no house facing a main street had windows or doors; sheltered side streets held the private entrances to homes.

Harappan citadels had thick walls and towers, with a marketplace as the central space. The Great Bath at Mohenjodaro citadel was 40 x 240 feet in dimension and was brick lined. Granaries were situated next to it. The entire city was built primarily of bricks made by baking the abundant clay of the Indus River Valley, a departure from the norm of dressed wood and stone, which was to be vaastu's leitmotif in later years.

But nothing in this very advanced city was quite so modern as the little-known matter of these urbanites having indoor toilets. There was a well-developed, covered sewage system, with deep channels to carry away the waste and stone manhole covers to access the subterranean channels. This was a level of sophistication that cities in India and the rest of the world would reach again only in the late nineteenth or early twentieth centuries. By 1500 B.C. the culture had disintegrated and the Harappans were forgotten. In 1915 ancient bricks from this long-forgotten "mound of the dead" were blithely used to build a railway embankment! By

1920 archaeologists had examined some of the seals casually tossed away in favor of more useful bricks, and they let out great yells of protest at this ignorant destruction of what was probably the first urban culture in the world. The bricks, over 3,000 years old, still hold up trains traversing them in Pakistan. Only the vaastu principles behind these cities survived.

Tracing the history of vaastu can quickly turn into a frustrating business, for India as a culture has relied heavily on the oral tradition, and until recently there was always an unspoken contemptuous pity for those whose memories required the aid of treated bark and stylus. Indeed there is a popular belief that most texts are written down in a period of decline in the subject they deal with, as a scramble to salvage fragments of knowledge before it is too late. Families held knowledge in trust and secrecy, and its transmission could be cut by a single untimely death. Knowledge and skill was diffused over a landmass the size of Europe. Many an ancient Indian heritage lived a precarious existence in the minds of irascible and cantankerous gurus who were perfectly prepared to die without parting with their treasures if they deemed no one worthy of such knowledge. (The oldest martial art of India and of the world, *kalaripayattu,* is on the verge of extinction today because the masters, at the turn of the twentieth century, refused to train what they perceived to be the wild and undisciplined youngsters of the time.) Add to such a scenario India's tradition of not caring much for history, and the difficulties become immense.

However, long before anything was set down in writing, vaastu principles were in operation and becoming part of the common currency. Today we know of some thirty-two ancient texts delineating the vaastu principles, all written between the fourth and twelfth centuries A.D. The texts have many features in common. There are detailed descriptions of the rules for building temples and carving the sculptures therein. Communities of people were divided according to occupations or caste groups; each group was accorded characteristic dwelling areas within city limits. Much ado was made about roads, entrances, exits, ventilation, and amount of sunlight received, with appropriate dire warnings for offending the deities who cluster in the earth. Major concerns included the site of construction, its soil and its nature, the laying of proper foundations, selecting appropriate construction materials, the tools required, and the qualities of the architect who alone could ensure rewarding construction on the site.

It was believed that prosperity and calmness of mind would inevitably result as a consequence of following these instructions. An excerpt from the *Vishwakarma Vaastushastra* exemplifies the attitudes of the texts.

By following the precepts of vaastu shastra, vigor, joy, and prosperity pervade the universe. Man attains the stature of the gods with this shastra.

He who knows this shilpa shastra knows also the
nature of all existence. They who follow vaastu
shastra gain the pleasures of the world and even
win through to heaven.

This is indeed a staggering level of confidence, yet considering the magnificent structures that were dotting the landscape
of India, such stalwart self-confidence is understandable.
However, history had a few nasty tricks up its sleeve. Beginning in the thirteenth century a series of invaders poured
across the north of India, powered by the fervid belief in
Islam and aghast at the seemingly endless sea of idolatry
before them. In those invasions the great library at Nalanda
was pillaged by destructive hordes. This event was cata-
strophic for the cultural heritage of India, for Nalanda was
the largest library and college in the world, drawing students
from all over Asia. What treasures of knowledge were lost in
that pillage is incalculable, but almost certainly the northern
traditions of vaastu were wiped out. Thus, almost all the
extant texts on the subject are from the south of India where,
until the fifteenth century, invasions were still vague rumors
from afar.

In fact, southern India was engaged in an energetic enter-
prise not usually associated with India—colonialism. The
priests of Buddhism and Hinduism fanned out across Southeast Asia, converting Thailand, Indonesia, Java, Sumatra, Bali,

Vietnam, and impacting even China and Japan. This was the period of greater India—a peaceful cultural conquest unparalleled in the bloody history of migration. Merchants, artisans, craftsmen, artists, and philosophers followed after the missionaries. So great was the export of talent that the greatest Hindu and Buddhist temples ever built are not found in India—these triumphs of vaastu are to be found in Angkor Wat and Borobudur, respectively (figure 3, page 16).

Alarmed at this relentless brain drain, the religious establishment enforced a prohibition against crossing the seas. Anybody who did so lost caste, which meant you were a living dead man. It also shut the door on any possible return for those who had left. Many vaastu masters were lost in this manner. With the destruction of the city of Vijaynagar in 1565, any high-culture agglomeration of vaastu texts and experts was lost forever.

By that time, in any case, the art had become sterile, stifled in the bonds of tradition, content with imitating the past and looking suspiciously on any heretical trends toward originality. Kerala, with its dense, tropical vegetation and distance from the usual invader routes, preserved this art well up to the twentieth century. Around 1934 the Mayamatam was rediscovered, along with a great many other classical texts, mainly Sanskrit plays.

A glance at the Mayamatam is enough to confirm the extent of the vaastu interests. Apart from the issues of the site, its examination, possession, orientation, and so on, the text draws elaborate vaastu grids and prescribes offerings to

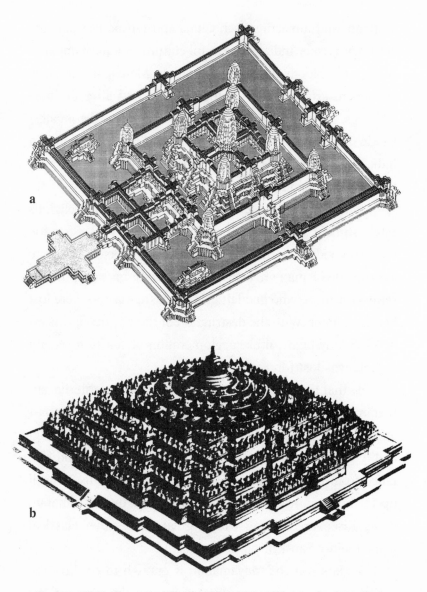

Figure 3. (a) Hindu temple of Angkor Wat; (b) Buddhist temple of Borobudur.

be made to the gods. Then it goes on to lay out the rules for establishing villages, enumerating eight specific types. There is the inevitable emphasis on caste and constructions based on caste regulations. For example, Brahmins and Kshatriyas (priests and warriors) should use baked bricks with mortar, Vaisyas and Shudras (traders and servants) should use unbaked bricks, and bamboo was open to all castes as a construction material.

The Mayamatam proceeds to describe town layouts, forts, marketplaces, and other features of urban life. There is a section on the number of stories in buildings and how to calculate their dimensions, what is to be laid as foundations, how pillars are constructed with various materials, and the choice of male, female, and neutral gender in bricks (!). One is soon in an ocean of detail.

Temples are described from one story to four and more, the living area for the temple staff is detailed, a large section on gateways is provided, and the same for pavilions and halls. Houses and royal palaces are covered in depth, and there is an interesting section on vehicles and their construction.

The traditional architect in the vaastu system was called the *shilpi* (the builder) or the *sthapathi* (he who puts in place). With the pride natural to all guilds, membership was limited (theoretically) to certain exceptional people possessing many desirable qualities. One typical example from the Mayamatam will suffice.

The architect is born in a land famed for this skill and he is free of any physical deformity. Being a superior person, he knows how to establish structures and is well versed in all the sciences. He is strong, imbued with justice and compassion, equanimous in mind, without jealousy and other weaknesses, handsome and astute in mathematics. He is learned in the ancient texts and about their authors. He is frank and sincere in his actions as he has controlled his sense organs. Drawing is his skill and he is acquainted with the geography of all lands. Greed is his undoing but he is known by his generosity. His health and energy are good and he is thus free of the seven deadly vices: abusive language, stealing property, acts of violence, hunting, gambling, wine, and women. His concentration and persistence are great and he bears proudly a distinguished well-chosen name; he easily crosses the ocean that is the science of architecture.

As to whether such an ideal paragon of virtues ever existed, the evidence is sketchy. Most folk stories deal with the theme of envious father shilpis being bested by upstart sons in the construction of some magnificent edifice—the son either remembering some abtruse formula the veteran forgets or providing the capstone for temples. It usually ends with the death of the son, either by suicide because he has mortified his father and thus disgraced the family in the eyes of the world, or by murder, with the young upstart being thrown off the top of the disputed structure. This is a theme that Daedelus, architect of the original Labyrinth in Greek mythology, and his nephew played out, too, so the archetype is strong.

Shilpis had three assistants. The first was the *sutra-grahin,* who was usually the son of the shilpi or his chief apprentice. His role was that of an on-site supervisor implementing the vision of the boss. He too knew the architectural arts and in a charming phrase is said to be able "to make the rope and rod fly" when measuring dimensions.

The *taksaka* is a mason and carpenter who does the actual carving, cutting, and dressing of material, whether wood, metal, or stone. Such worked material is assembled, under the guidance of the sutragrahin, by the *vardhaki.* This distinction seems a bit superfluous, but such roles were assigned by hereditary occupational castes, and nobody would dream of overstepping the limits of one's traditional role. It also created a traditional reluctance to indulge in physical labor among the upper castes, because there were specific lower castes to do all that sweaty stuff!

The shilpi, sutragrahin, taksaka, and vardhaki form a

tetrad, the four points of the square, providing stability to structures. We always come back to the square in vaastu, though this by no means implies a construction team of just four. The number is philosophically pleasing and practically expedient. The architect or shilpi is also revered symbolically as standing in for Vishwakarma, the cosmic architect of the gods, and he had a respect and deference paid to him that was quite remarkable. A house with bad vaastu was a disaster, a guarantee of deaths, poverty, disease, strife, childlessness, and unfaithful women. Only the Vishwakarma substitute could prevent this disaster and assure prosperity.

The tools of the architect—the *sutrastaka*—were simple (figure 4). Eight in number, they consisted first of a scale marked off in angulas. Then there was a triangular-shaped level, rope, a plumb line, and a dividers compass, along with a square and reference marker. But the most important tool of the sutrastaka was the human eye. Everything had to look just right, even if it had been measured to formalistic satisfaction. A good vaastu architect, in fact, becomes unusually alert and aware of his surroundings, sensing defects and flaws in construction long before the measuring tapes are out. The insistence that the eye be the primary tool of the trade keeps this ideal well developed.

An interesting concept vaastu shares with scuplture proper is that all work begins from the *nabhi,* or navel. The process of carving an idol is always begun from the navel, and the construction on a site also begins from the navel of the Vaastu Purusha we have met before. The navel is sup-

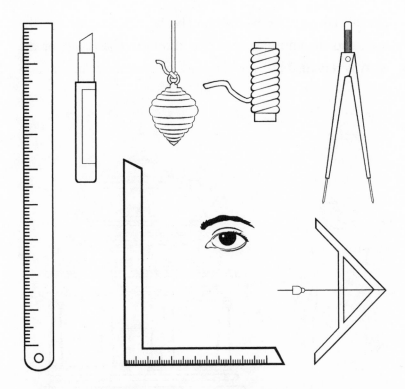

Figure 4. The vaastu architect's tools.

posed to be the loci of creative energies, the stable point of a body. Because each image represents the Yupa Stambha, the Axis Mundi, or Pillar of the Universe, great care and concern were always taken before work began.

These ideas eventually expanded into the concept of the temple being representative of the Purusha, cosmic man. In this context, every part of a well-designed vaastu temple fits into a particular section of the human body. The top of the temple is the head, the sanctum corresponds to the neck, the assembly hall is the stomach. The boundary walls are the legs, and the entrance serves as the feet. The image of the deity is regarded as the vital spark of soul, the *Jiva,* that ani-

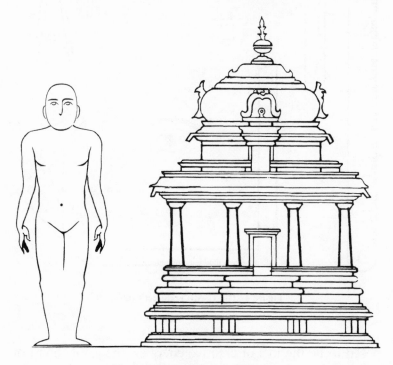

Figure 5. The temple as cosmic man.

mates the entire temple-body (figure 5).

The idea of the temple being a representation of the human body is neither original nor unique to India. The temples of Greece and Egypt were based on similar principles. In his brilliant work *The Temple of Man,* the Egyptologist R. A. Schwaller de Lubicz shows that every detail of the Temple of

Luxor is designed to reflect the cosmos in the form of man. As in vaastu, the temples of Egypt were based on the rectangle, however the cosmic man was vertical in vaastu, reaching up to the spire of the temple, while in Egypt the man was laid out horizontally, the entire complex becoming the body and the sanctum usually located where the heart of this primal man would be (figure 6). Since the Egyptians

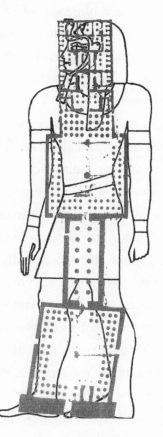

Figure 6. The vertical cosmic man.

considered the heart to be the seat of the soul, this was very similar to the vaastu practice of the *sanctum sanctorum* housing the Jiva, the soul of the temple-body.

In a common practice with feng shui, vaastu placed great emphasis on appropriate locations for temples. Eventually the knowledge gained from these endeavors began to be applied to the mundane needs of housing for ordinary people. Favored sites were hills, riverbanks, seashores, forests with light vegetation, confluences of rivers, groves of trees, and sites made sacred by the inhabitation of saints. These are *siddha* locations, good and approved. Towns and villages are *asiddha,* necessary concessions to people's needs and the imperatives of history.

A peculiar aspect of the rediscovery of the ancient temple sites of India deserves a closer look for the light it casts on the beliefs of ancient India. Most temples that were discovered were overgrown with vegetation. This was not merely because of the prolific forest reclaiming what was abandoned or ruined, but, it soon became apparent to the startled archaeologists, this was actually designed to occur.

Once a completed temple was consecrated, trees would be planted all around it as well as within the courtyard. By a vast majority two types of trees emerge the favorites: the banyan *(Ficus benghalensis)* and the peepal *(Ficus religiosa).* Both these trees have very deep roots in the religious culture of India, the peepal—as its name implies—being considered a spiritual tree. The banyan is the favored tree of meditating sages, as well as all manner of supernatural residents in the abundant mythology of the country. Both of them grow rapidly, the banyan sending out roots at an alarming rate while the peepal scatters its seeds in a profligate manner, taking root almost at will.

The builders of these temples were wise and did not have the hubris to expect their structures to endure forever. The last words of the Buddha have permeated the mind of India as has nothing else—"Decay is inherent in all things that come into being"—and so these temples were designed to revert to a natural state once their usefulness had expired. As long as the temples were spiritual centers of the community, providing succor and solace to the souls of the faithful, the complexes would be well maintained. Cleanliness would ensure that seeds could not nestle into tiny cracks, and the roots of the banyan would be turned aside.

But when discord seized the temple community, when indifference replaced faith and bickerings were heard more frequently than prayers, the roots would begin to snake inward to the complex. Subtly, relentlessly, they would swallow up the now dying temple. These trees were the dark spot of yin within the white creative light of yang, ever ready to expand when the light waned.

The peepal tree is also symbolic of inevitable destruction. When the cycle of ages culminates in the cataclysm of water, the peepal leaf alone will float on the water, bearing upon it Lord Vishnu. It is a constant reminder of inevitable doom, a doom hastened by evil actions and hence to be guarded against.

It is by no means an accident that in India almost all the temples built as a monument to some ruler's ego, or trader's wealth, ended up claimed by the jungle and eke out shadowy existences as tourist sites today, valuable as archaeological artifacts, not spiritual centers. And all those humble shrines erected for the greater glory of God—they thrive.

As we can see, vaastu was clearly a dominant part of India's culture for some time, and its relative obscurity in recent times owes much to the loss of the key texts. While it is gratifying to see vaastu being discovered in the United States, it is even more exciting to see the fervor with which it has been reembraced by its homeland. Let us now take a more in-depth look at the actual practice of vaastu.

2
KEY ELEMENTS OF VAASTU

Like many other ancient cultures, the Indians divided the primal elements into five—earth, water, fire, air, and ether. The ideas can be traced back to the Samkhya philosophers of the eighth century B.C. According to this system the primal void condenses into ether (or the element space). Ether in turn condenses into air. From air is born fire, which in turn transmutes into water. Water's final transformation is into earth. Earth therefore is the most complex of all the elements, the culmination and fulfillment of the process of genesis.

As each element unfolds or manifests itself, a parallel sense function arises to perceive it. Hearing perceives ether, touch perceives air, sight views fire, taste evolves with water, and finally, smell comes into being with earth. Each of these elements is also assigned a characteristic color and shape. Ether is yellow and shaped like a dot—the *bindu* that adorns the forehead of Hindu women (and a growing number of American teenagers) even today. Air is a circle, green with its promise of life-giving rain. The circle symbolizes the bounded space that encircles us all; any mountaintop provides this vision of sky. The circle, then, is the space within which we live; the dot is the cosmos around that.

Fire is a red triangle, its rigid geometry signifying man's conscious effort to impact his environment so that life becomes easier. A blue crescent symbolizes water, perhaps a collective unconscious memory of the association between the moon and tides. It all coalesces into the orange or saffron square of earth. (Saffron has always been the most spiritually esteemed color in India.) The square—and its variant, the cube—is the most stable geometric structure. It is the unvarying basis for all vaastu construction.

Of course as a consequence houses or their sites could not be shaped in circles, crescents, or triangles. These shapes are extremely ill regarded in vaastu thought. It is easy to see why the science has misgivings about building structures on air (circular shape), fire (triangle), or water (crescents). This is asking for disaster, an invitation to chastise hubris.

In all of this, the point must not be overlooked that the

28

bindu, ether, is the inevitable underlying material out of which everything is made, including houses. Thus the central spot of the vaastu grid, called the *brahmasthana,* houses that bindu, the "seed out of which forms grow." This spot is the spiritual and energy center of the structure and usually houses the sanctum sanctorum in temples, or sacred plants in the courtyard of a house.

Another reason for the choice of the square has to do with the theory of *gunas,* qualities inherent in people, analogous to the "humors" of medieval Europe. *Tamas,* the quality of inertness, is represented by the circle. *Rajas,* the quality of taking action, is represented by the octagon and sometimes by the triangle. *Sattwa,* the quality of harmony with one's self, is represented by the square. Obviously, harmony is a highly prized quality in a household. If you cannot have a square, a rectangle is an acceptable substitute, its resident energies being considered to be almost as stable and harmonizing. This is a matter of immense practical consequence. Rectangular plots of land are the norm in vaastu, and all deviations from the ideal are sought to be solved by somehow making the site a rectangle in symbolic terms.

THE PRIME IMPORTANCE OF DIRECTION

In chilly Europe, you "make hay while the sun shines." If there is any time left over, you then bask in the sun. In tropical India on the other hand you "flourish in the shade." A great compliment to pay a person is to say that people have been "living in his shade," for it implies a caring and protective attitude. A few degrees of heat can contribute to vast differences between cultures. Vaastu makes much ado about proper directional siting of structures because it is always grappling with that scorching Indian reality, the sun.

It is for this reason that nonfunctional rooms, such as storerooms, are recommended for the SW sector. Peak exposure to the sun's rays occurs in the afternoon, when the sun is in the SW. Thus vaastu cautions to avoid placing rooms there that you are likely to spend large amounts of time in. One recommendation is to grow a tree in the SW sector—to diffuse the effects of concentrated sun, though this is not always explained. As with other ancient traditions, what was originally perfectly sound advice becomes, over time, something carried on ritually with no remnant understanding of the reasons for doing such.

Similarly, vaastu does not recommend sleeping with your head to the N. This experiment can be tried out by anybody and is certain to produce erratic and disturbed sleep. The reason? The body's natural magnetism repels the alike poles of force generated by the earth's magnetic field. This is good common sense, as is the advice to sleep facing E: early light falling on eyelids triggers a waking response in the body, allowing one to arise feeling refreshed and energetic.

Another vaastu preoccupation is with the direction of air flow. This can be a real problem in the north of India where the hot "loo" winds blow, adding to misery, not reliev-ing it. Vaastu houses were designed so that most activity would be centered around the courtyard, where open spaces gave fresh air but were also buffered from the hot winds. Vaastu tenets are also quite specific about the size of win-dows in walls—they have to be large enough to allow the free flow of air, but not so large that the hot sun or wind would roast the inhabitants within.

ORIENTING THE SITE

The first step for any vaastu architect is to orient the site within the vaastu grid. Traditionally, the ritual known as *shankustaapana* (literally, "fixing the conch shell") was used to determine the navel of the Vaastu Purusha in the site, which is usually slightly off the geometric center (figure 7, page 32). The ritual involves some exceedingly complicated procedures involving drawing circles and measuring shad-ows to determine the cardinal points. It requires extensive training and has long been regarded as the most tricky part of the entire business of building a house. Only the most experienced and confident stapathi would actually do the shankustaapana, for if anything went wrong later, he was to shoulder the blame! Nowadays a compass will suffice for most people, except for extreme traditionalists.

Vaastu has always been particularly attentive to the height of a building; vertical proportions are regarded as

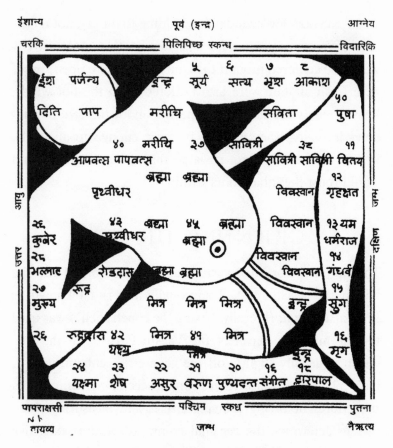

**Figure 7. The traditional Vaastu Purusha layout,
with the navel off-center.**

having great aesthetic significance. The Mayamatam lists
some of the desirable proportions as follows:

Shaantika—Peaceful. The height is equal to the
breadth. This is a very harmonious and soothing
structure, especially easy on the eye.

Paustika—Replete. The height is 1.25 times the
breadth. This is associated with strength,
eminence, and completion.

Jayada—Victory (or joy) giver. The height is 1.5
times the breadth.

Sarva Kaamika—Fulfillment of all desires. The
height is 1.75 times the breadth.

Adhbuta—The marvellous. The height is twice the
breadth. The building is supposed to inspire
wonder and awe in the beholder because of its
gorgeousness.

THE CENTRAL POSITION
OF THE GRID

The Vaastu Purusha mandala, or the vaastu grid, is theoretically the most important aspect of vaastu. Within the grid
sit the forty-five deities and minor gods who assaulted the
Vaastu Purusha. Usually a grid consists of a central open
space, a built-up area around it, an open space around that,
and then a compound wall, as shown in figure 8 (page 34).
Since each god is a particular function of nature, the allot-
ment and uses of the house are decided accordingly. For
example, section 9, the SE corner, is the place of Agni, the
god of fire. Accordingly, the kitchen range is recommended
to be placed here. The NE corner, the face of Vaastu
Purusha, is left unbuilt; at most a body of water could go

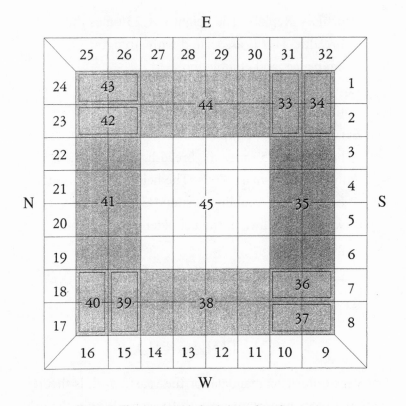

Figure 8. The vaastu grid, divided into forty-five sections.

here. Bathrooms are usually placed in the W sector, guarded by Varuna, the god of water.

The spot of Brahma in the center should always be kept vacant. Having even a pool of water there is regarded as a misfortune, and a toilet is an absolute calamity. Usually the space is left free, or a sacred Tulsi plant is placed there.

3

THE IMPORTANCE
OF ENVIRONMENT

Before a house is built or selected, vaastu recommends that you check out the worthiness of the environment. Taking up residence near a graveyard, crematorium, or cemetery is to be avoided. Quite apart from the nuisance of funeral processions, there is the matter of the psychological costs one pays to be so constantly reminded of mortality. Most people are not up to it. There is also the association of crematorium grounds with tantric black magic rites that makes such a site distasteful to vaastu.

Vaastu practitioners carefully note the direction in which a site slopes. A slope toward the E provides overall well-being. A slope toward the N is a wealth generator, as Kubera, lord of wealth, lives there. A W slope is inimical to knowledge, and a S-descending slope is traditionally extremely bad news. In general the N-S axis of the site should be the larger side of the rectangle.

Water flowing along the W and S sides of a property is ill regarded for the long-term prospects of those inhabiting the site. But a river flowing in the NE direction is a vaastu dream come true. Several ashrams have developed along such a natural feature.

Prominent natural features such as rocks, hills, mounds, or large boulders can be safely left in place if they are on the S, SW, or W sides of the plot. "Heavy" objects are preferred here; they block the late afternoon sun. Remove them if they fall in any of the other sectors. If that is not feasible, avoid that site. This is in sharp contrast to feng shui, which prefers an armchair shape—hills in the north and "arms" on the E and W, with a hillock on the south side and even a stream flowing by the "footstool." A vaastu expert would have a fit if confronted with such a site. See chapter 8 for a detailed comparison of the two systems.

Religious structures within the plot or site are well regarded or at least tolerated. Outside your boundaries, they cast heavy shadows on your fortunes. The energies of the site all get focused on this religious magnet, which might explain why temple towns and pilgrim towns never really become anything else. The same issue of a dwelling's energies being drawn off by a powerful neighboring structure means you shouldn't build near schools, cinemas, and so on.

Any sort of ruin (or dilapidated structure aspiring to become a ruin) near your site is to be avoided. In India, historical apathy has ensured that ruins are never regarded as picturesque, just nuisances. Even the homeless avoid them.

But do not despair! All these obstacles are rendered powerless if between them and your site runs a public road! And if the distance between the bringers of bad luck and you is over twice the height of your house, that's good news too. We see here an obvious compromise forced upon the vaastu tribe by the pressures of population and relative lack of inhabitable space.

In the tradition of good fences making good neighbors, vaastu advocates a respectful distance from other houses. Rainwater should not flow from neighbors' roofs onto your plot, particularly in the NE sector. Like rocks and boulders, neighbors' high-rises are welcome if they occupy the S, SW, or W sides of your plot, but are bad luck if they block the NE.

An important point to keep in mind is that the NE sector should be free of any electrical transformers or electrical poles.

The ideal plot is aligned with the magnetic lines of force. A deviance of 15 to 30 degrees is tolerated—otherwise few plots indeed would be habitable! When the four corners of a site synchronize with the cardinal points of the compass, this is called *vidishi*. This rare situation creates an area of neutral or dead energy. The solution is the placement of the main door. If that is accurate, then the disrupted energy field becomes functional again. (The position of doors is explained in The House Proper, chapter 5. Also see Auspicious Times, chapter 7).

You should never put yourself into the position of being enclosed on either side by sites that are larger than yours. The same prohibition applies to buildings that are larger than your own—they loom as tokens of poverty in your future life.

Swimming pools or wells that neighbors possess to your SE, SW, or NW sink you. They are acceptable in the NE, E, or N.

If such constructions come up after you have built your house, try to persuade the owners to change their plans. You can also take countermeasures. Screens that block off the offending sight are an option that is rapidly gaining popularity in India, though there is still a hardy flock that prefers the national sport—litigation. The trivial causes that lead to construction litigation are beyond belief. Litigation is also unwise from a vaastu standpoint, in fact vaastu is against any association with a plot or site that has a history of acrimonious litigation behind it. Court-auctioned land should be avoided at all costs.

PROPER SOIL SELECTION

Vaastu places a great deal of importance on the proper quality of soil at the site for a house. An initial test of sorts is to dig two pits of the dimensions 2 feet by 2 feet by 2 feet. Care must be taken that the soil of the two pits is not mixed together. In one of these pits the soil should be put back. Once the pit is filled, there should be a residue of soil left over. If the dug-up soil exactly packs the pit or, even worse, falls short, then the site is not regarded as being productive of prosperity.

The other pit is to be filled to the brim with water. In an ideal site, the water should take over an hour to be absorbed by the soil. If it takes less time than that, the site is regarded as a potential drain on resources. Large cracks left behind in the pit after the water drains away is a forewarning of extensive construction expenses. A couple small cracks is not a matter of concern; if there are more than seven cracks, watch out.

A quicker test of soil quality is to dig the pit, fill it with water, and walk away for a length of 100 paces at your normal gait. When you return, a good site will retain over half the water, an average site between one-fourth and one-half the water, and a poor site less than one-fourth.

Black soil that goes down to a depth of twelve feet is supposed to be an obstacle that no amount of hard work can overcome. One's career and progress in life stagnate. Black soil that covers the first three to four feet and is upon a layer of white or red soil is fine. White is considered the best color for soil, followed by red. Yellowish soil is regarded as very beneficial for people in business. If the soil is crumbly and friable, this indicates an easy and steady cash flow. Soil that exudes an oily or pleasant smell within one foot of digging is also well regarded.

Should you have no option but to build on a site with unsuitable soil, there is still a remedy that you can take, though it is rather drastic. Remove wholesale the first six feet of soil from the site and fill it up with suitable soil from elsewhere! This is actually done in India, expenses be damned. Sometimes it is done by the wealthy as a safety pre-caution, because of the fear that within the soil will be found lurking inauspicious or fortune-destroying objects. These include iron and steel pieces, animal bones, eggshells, and, of course, human bones. These are, unfortunately, far more likely to be found than the traditional good luck objects— cow horns, copper pieces, gold or silver coins, or ancient bricks.

VEGETATION ON THE SITE

Vegetation in India tends to be like that found in other trop-ical climates—thick, fecund, and eager to expand. Any homeowner knows the destructive effect all these roots and creepers can have on walls and foundations. Monsoons tend to bring trees crashing down dangerously, and things that crawl and bite in the underbrush can't help but wander into nearby houses. Many Indian towns have had a long and respectfully tense relationship with the snakes that abound in the villages. For all these reasons, vaastu traditionally recommends clearing all vegetation from a building site. Thorny trees and those exuding sticky sap are particularly to be avoided. One vaastu text even worries, charmingly, that the many flowering plants and their intoxicating perfumes will distract the mind of the good citizen from his stern round of duty!

Today, with deforestation a much greater global concern than poisonous snakes, we certainly don't want to eliminate vegetation that isn't a problem. Vaastu is about living in optimum harmony with the environment, not making a sterile attempt at control that seems more like a scorched-earth policy than architectural design. As with all other rules in vaastu, one's good judgment should guide the ultimate decision. One rule of thumb is to accommodate whatever trees exist, unless they are found in the NE sector or the exact center of the vaastu grid. This strikes a nice balance between hardcore vaastu tenets and common sense. One should always keep in mind a saying attributed to Maharishi Ganga: "Wherever the mind finds happiness and the eyes derive pleasure, man should reside there."

A last concern is the height of respective sectors of the site. This is usually not applicable to those living in multistoried apartment complexes, as everything has been leveled out. But for those in the country, as a general rule the W, SW, and S should be higher than the other sectors and the land should slope toward the E, NE, and N. In such circumstances plots that are cut or lacking land area in the SE, S, SW, and NW sectors are quite welcome.

THE SITE 4 PROPER

Vaastu has an overwhelming preference for sites that
are either square or rectangular in shape, no matter
what their size. Most vaastu recommendations for alter-
ing a site are essentially ways of transforming the existing
site of land to bring it closer to that ideal state of stability
represented by the square and rectangle. Figure 9a on page
44 shows the absolute ideal shape. Rectangles are fine too,
provided they are of a ratio of 1:2 and not more, whether it
be length or breadth (figure 9b).

Any extensions to the intrinsic square shape are well

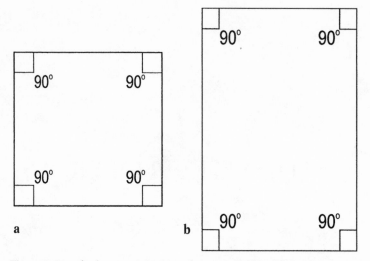

Figure 9. A perfectly square site (a) and a rectangle (b) with a ratio of 1:1.5.

regarded only in the sections north, east, and northeast. That area corresponds to the face and neck of the Vaastu Purusha, and "increase in face" is welcome. Any other projections beyond the confines of the rectangle are regarded as deforming the body of the Vaastu Purusha.

Triangular and circular site shapes are, as previously mentioned, inherently unstable because of their elemental association with fire and air. Five-cornered sites are regarded as being conducive to harsh-minded and vicious scheming— more than one vaastu person has pointed to the Pentagon's penchant for getting embroiled in overseas conflict. Before it was built America lived in splendid, and well-liked, international isolation.

The *gomukhi,* or cow-faced site, (figure 10) is auspicious. In this site the front area is distinctly smaller than the

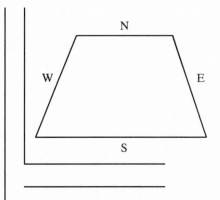

Figure 10. The gomukhi, or cow-faced site.

rear. Roads on this site must run on the S or W sides only, otherwise problems will arise for other reasons and the benefits of the site will be lost.

The tiger-faced site, or *vyaagramukhi*, (figure 11, page 46) is the reverse of the cow-faced site, with the front area being broad and voracious, like the open jaws of the tiger, and the rear being compact. This will cause the owner to become unpleasant and rapacious.

The royal Mayan city of Copan, circa A.D. 600–800, occupied a tiger-faced site. It had a river flowing to the S, which from a vaastu perspective takes good fortune flowing away. The NE sector was unnecessarily built up and had no open space within it, or even a river or lake within it, which is again against the tenets of vaastu. The city rapidly overpopulated itself, stripped the forest, and exhausted its agricultural soil. These are all classical problems with tiger-faced

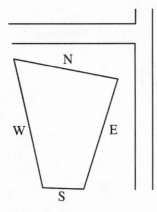

Figure 11. The vyaagramukhi, or tiger-faced site.

sites, and it can be very instructive to note how vaastu tenets hold true an entire world away.

Hexagons, octagons, and irregular parallelograms are not desirable. All irregular and odd shapes need to be divided or modified so that they more closely approximate a square or rectangle. For example, figure 12 shows a site with a chunk missing from the N side. The owner should attempt to purchase the "missing" land that will complete the

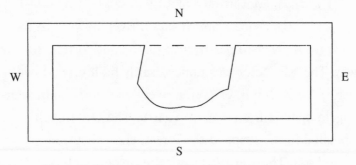

Figure 12. Rectangular site with an irregularity on one side.

rectangle. The only exception to this "squaring off" is when the building or structure protrudes into the N or E of the NE sector, as shown in figure 13. This is considered beneficial and can be left as is.

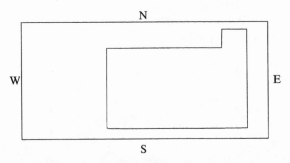

Figure 13. A site with an acceptable spur in the northeast sector.

In the case where your site has an unwanted protrusion, it can be rectified by isolating the offending section with a compound wall or hedge. By doing so you basically "pretend" that the protrusion is not a part of your site. Your goal can be either a perfect square or rectangle, or a site with the desirable NE spur, as in figure 14 (page 48).

Let us now take a look at some common site shapes and compare their benefits and the uses to which each can be put.

Circular sites can be used in exceptional circumstances if there is a perfectly circular public building on it. To build a square or rectangular building on such a site is an open invitation to disaster. Many vaastu experts feel that even a circular building on such a site does not mitigate the inherent difficulties of such places. However, let it be said that

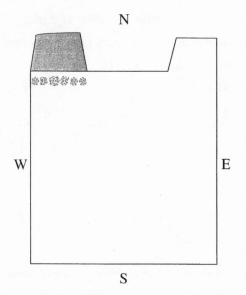

Figure 14. Using a hedge to eliminate an undesirable spur.

feng shui is of exactly the other opinion—a perfectly round site is avidly sought after in that system.

In any case, it is rather rare to stumble across a site of land shaped like a perfect circle. The chariot wheel site, an irregular circle (figure 15), is more common. Like the perfect circle, it is universally rejected as being inimical to prosperity and one's social status.

Sites shaped like irregular parallelograms (figure 16) have all their sides of different dimensions. Unless one is prepared to spend an inordinate amount of money straightening this out, it is best to avoid such a site.

The triangular shape (figure 17), whether equilateral or uneven, is not well regarded. Traditionally it is supposed to

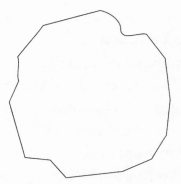

Figure 15. The chariot wheel site.

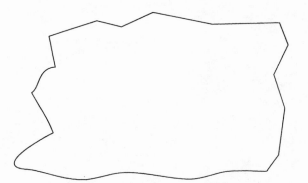
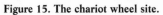

Figure 16. The irregular parallelogram site.

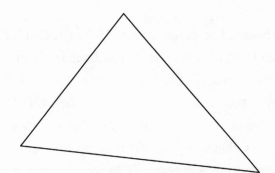

Figure 17. The triangle site.

involve the owner in litigation with government, and bring all one's plans to a frustrating impasse.

The *bhadrasana* shape (figure 18), named after a yogic posture, is useful for specialized buildings such as museums and research centers. It is of absolutely no use for residential buildings. Obviously, the chances of coming into possession of such a peculiarly shaped piece of land is not high, though in India you will occasionally find one, a legacy of ancient rock-cut architecture.

Figure 18. The bhadrasana site.

The distorted rectangle (figure 19), a site that looks like a rail or steel bar, having all length and negligible breadth, is a fairly common shape. Pressures of space see a great many schools and office complexes built on such sites. That is a pragmatic use of space, but vaastu remains uneasy about it.

A cleaver shape (figure 20) is of no real value as it is; once the protrusion is choked off, however, using one of the methods of rectification, the site makes a perfect rectangle.

Similarly, a flag-shaped sight (figure 21) can easily be rectified to make a perfect rectangle.

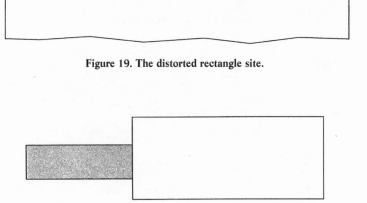

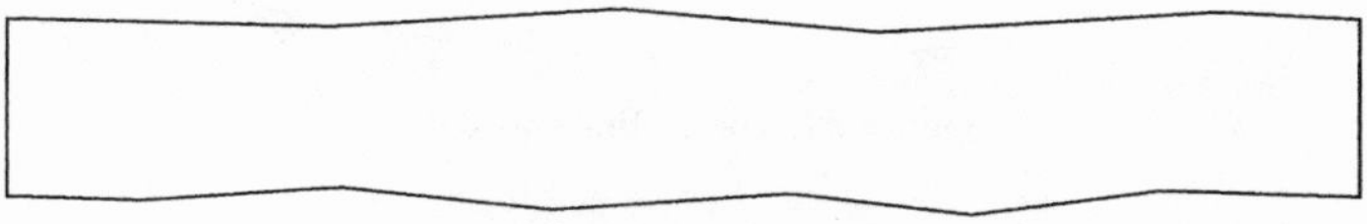

Figure 19. The distorted rectangle site.

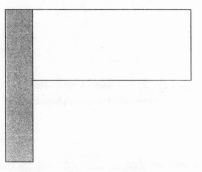

Figure 20. The cleaver-shaped site.

Figure 21. The flag-shaped site.

A coffin-shaped site (figure 22, page 52), unsurprisingly, is inimical to the health of family members.

There are two variations on the drum-shaped site (figure 23 a and b, page 52) and both are ill regarded. The

Figure 22. The coffin-shaped site.

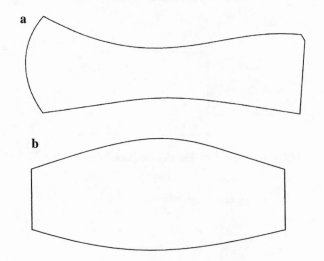

Figure 23. (a) The damaru drum-shaped site, and
(b) the dholak drum-shaped site.

damaru, or concave drum, is regarded as being the cause of eye troubles for people living on it, while the *dholak,* the convex drum, has negative effects upon the women of the family in particular. The underlying philosophical reason for this unease is quite interesting. In the Indian aesthetic tradition stringed instruments represent the creative function.

Wind instruments represent the nourishing aspects of life, as in Krishna's flute or Vishnu's conch shell. Percussion instruments represent the destructive forces of the universe, as represented in the damaru of Shiva, the little drum that relentlessly thrums out the entropy time brings to all things. Every classical musical performance combines these three elements as an acknowledgment of the symbiosis of forces that constitute the universe. The unease over these drum-shaped sites is actually the fear of getting in the path of the relentless forces of destruction, of foolishly accelerating the decay inherent in all material things.

A site vaguely resembling a turtle or a wooden paddle (figure 24) is credited with causing all manner of disasters: murder, imprisonment, and untimely death being but some of the gloomy tidings. Fortunately very rare, this shape should be avoided like the plague.

Figure 24. The turtle-shaped site.

A winnow separates grain from chaff, and a winnow-shaped site (figure 25, page 54) will separate owners from their wealth and peace of mind with impressive efficiency. Avoid this kind of site at all costs.

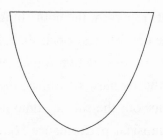

Figure 25. The winnow-shaped site.

A bow-shaped site (figure 26)—any site that has a straight side faced by a curved one—is accompanied by an increased chance of burglary.

A bullet-shaped site (figure 27)—either a bar with a curved side or an oval-shaped site that is abruptly cut off—attracts enmity and causes loss of friendship, but it can be rectified into a rectangle without too many hassles and hence is a manageable shape.

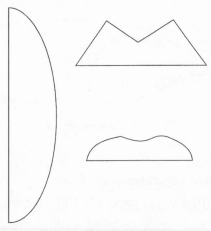

Figure 26. Bow-shaped sites.

Figure 27. The bullet-shaped site.

A basket-shaped site (figure 28) can be rectified into a square or rectangle, but a large amount of space is wasted in the process and it is probably better to continue searching for a better site.

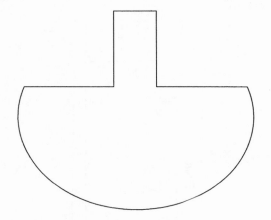

Figure 28. The basket-shaped site.

There are, of course, an unlimited number of possible shapes for plots of land. Using the guidelines for the shapes I have discussed—basically, trying to achieve rectangles as easily as possible—you should be able to make a basic evaluation of the appropriateness for any piece you come across.

ROADS

The position of roads in relation to your site is a key consideration. Sites having roads on all four sides are the best (figure 29). Roads in the N and E are best, and more than one road is preferable, because movement along them cancels out negative energies that might otherwise flow to you. S and W roads are beneficial for people in business life. S and E side roads are also good for organizations dealing with

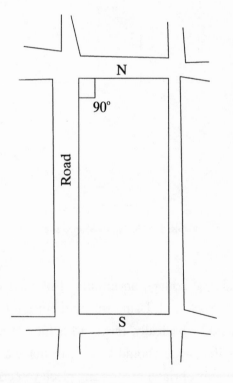

Figure 29. Having roads on all four sides of a site is beneficial.

women's issues. Roads in the N and E must always be lower than those running in the S or W. Since the site itself should also have higher elevations on the S and W, the roads usually follow.

A stream, instead of a road, that runs from NW to E is a very good substitute for ideal road placement.

Sites that have corners rounded off because of a road's curve need to be rectified into a square. The exception to this is a rounded corner in the SE, which can be lived with.

Once the issue of the selection of a site is over, we can move on to the house that will be built upon it, which forms the substance of our next chapter.

5
THE HOUSE PROPER

When dealing with the issue of the ideal vaastu house, it helps to remember a fundamental rule. Vaastu has a fixed ideal design for any structure that humans use, and efforts at construction are attempts to realize that ideal. This is applied without exception. The structure could be a free-standing house, a multistoried flat structure, office spaces, or educational institutions. A few variations exist for special cases and they are covered in the next chapter: Industrial and Commercial Vaastu. For the vast majority of structures, however, including single-family homes, vaastu has a system and it adheres to it.

This makes vaastu unusually easy to follow as a guide. Once the basic grid layout is grasped, the principles can be extrapolated across a variety of circumstances, situations, and structures. (Chapter 9 provides a quick run-through of these basic rules, to be used as a ready-reference as needed).

Figure 30 shows an idealized house design. It is rectangular and has all the classical features. This is the key grid for all vaastu planning, thus it should be memorized. It gives you three choices for bedrooms, with the SW corner being the best, then the NW, and finally the W, plus an E guest room. In Indian tradition, the bedroom on the W sector was known as the "room for sulking." The wife would lie down in there when she wanted her husband to know that he was in the doghouse, and it was expedient on his part to initiate a serious reconciliation effort. Because women were traditionally submissive in that culture, this was a socially sanctioned method to ensure that they still had some influence. Nowadays the children's bedroom is often placed there, and a fair amount of sulking still goes on.

The NE ought to be the lowest spot of the site or structure. It is reserved for rooms of worship, reception or waiting areas, or for water bodies of all sorts. One feng shui tip that fits well with vaastu's tenets is to have a fish tank in the NE with nine goldfish inside. The results can be startlingly close to magic.

The central space is known as the Brahmasthana, after the creator god who sat upon the Vaastu Purusha. A skylight is a great advantage here. This central space must stay

NW   N   NE

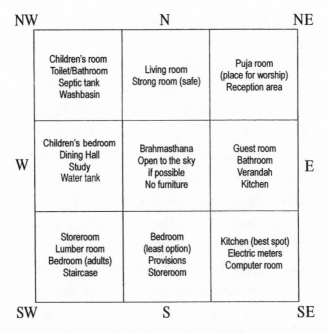

SW   S   SE

Figure 30. An ideal vaastu house grid design.

absolutely uncluttered. Vaastu consultants are rigid about this. Any sort of structure, even a fish bowl, is oppressive of your fortune. A TV or stereo here is akin to an energy volcano, bringing cataclysm to the household, while a fireplace or woodstove quite literally becomes one. Leave the Brahmasthana stark and bare. A carpet would be the only allowable item.

The SW and W are the areas where the heavy furnishing should go. Weight in these sectors is regarded as an immense advantage. If possible they should be the highest points of the house, thus extra floors to a building that don't cover the entire structure are best placed here. Any overhead tanks should be positioned here for the "weight" factor.

The SE sector is ruled by fire, so it is the best choice for the kitchen. Electrical and electronic equipment is also considered to be part of the fire element, so the SE can make a good spot for the computer room as well. If possible, place your electric meter on this corner. (Note, however, that power lines above the house or crossing your open space within the vaastu grid are a source of ill fortune. They should be shifted or buried so that they do not cross the house.)

The study and the meditation room fall in the W for the interesting reason that one should face E, the direction of light and knowledge, when meditating or thinking deeply, and there should be as much open space as possible in front of you to allow the light and knowledge to cover you. Placing the study in the W puts the open central space directly to the E.

With regard to the materials used in vaastu construction, there is a traditional preference for natural materials, wood being by far the favorite. However materials in themselves do not greatly affect vaastu structures. The rules are simple. Use new material as far as possible. New construction needs new materials. Recycled materials are acceptable for repair work. Vaastu carefully differentiates between what is antique and what is old. Antique is fine, old is not. The formal definition of antique in India is anything over one hundred years in age.

THE LIVING ROOM

Ideal positions for the living room are in the N or E sectors. Doors should be positioned on the E or W sides of the room. Chandeliers ought not to be in the geometrical center but skewed slightly to the W. Rooms have Brahmasthanas as well as do houses, and preventing the center of the room from being laden with "weight" is the logic behind this asymmetric recommendation.

Disturbing portraits or works of art depicting war, devastation by natural forces, human misery, or predacious animals are to be avoided, because of their obvious negative energy. Many martial artists, however, will hang up a picture of their power animal, a spirit force they seek to emulate. Even if you are not a martial artist, hanging artwork that depicts scenes or "energies" that you wish to emulate can be

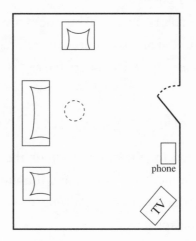

Figure 31. The living room.

conducive to happiness. No religious icons or photos should be placed above the entrance doors.

TVs are ideally placed in the SE corner of the living room (the corner ruled by fire). They should not be placed in the NE or SW. Telephones can be in the E or SE but not in the SW, NW, or N. One should not have liquids of any sort near a telephone or TV, no juices, no drinks, no beverages, no water pipes, and so forth. Water is opposed to fire, and they thus tend to interfere with one another. I have personally witnessed this shifting of a telephone away from a water cooler to benefit a businessman who needed to be more effective with his phone time. He has been happy with the results.

As with the house itself, vaastu prefers square or rectangular shapes in furniture, for reasons of stability and balance. Chairs and couches should be arranged along the E, W, and N sides. If you don't want to get up for calls, you'd better get a cordless phone.

Preferable colors for the living room are white, yellow, blue, and green. Red and black are not well regarded for this room, as they carry negative, angry energy.

THE DINING ROOM

The ideal location for the dining room is the W. The E and N are acceptable too. The kitchen and dinning space should never be on different floors. Carrying food up and down stairs is very inauspicious.

The best direction to face when dining is E. The head

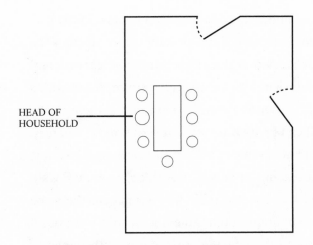

Figure 32. The dining room.

of the family should sit facing this direction. Others can face
E, W, or N, but avoid facing S, the direction of death. Fold-
ing tables lack stability and should not be used for dining.
Square or rectangular tables are best.

Articles over the door are not recommended for this
room. The door can be in the E, N, or W. There should never
be a bathroom attached to the dinning room; Hinduism
places much emphasis on enforcing physical and mental
space between places for food and for elimination. Suggested colors are light blue, light green, or pale yellow.

THE KITCHEN

It is quite important to place the kitchen—with its range,
toaster oven, microwave oven, and electrical devices—in the

fire corner of the house, the SE. Having a kitchen in the N is regarded as an inducement to become extravagant. The range should be located in the SE corner of the kitchen, and other electrical devices, such as the refrigerator, should be as close to the SE corner as possible. *Do not* put them in the SW. The S wall can be used for the cupboard and the pantry.

One should always face E when preparing food, so it is practical to place counters and butcher blocks on the E wall, near the range. If there is a table in the kitchen, the same rules apply as to a dining room table: the head of the household faces E, with others facing any direction other than S. When serving food, however, one should face W. A kitchen table near the W wall fulfills all these requirements.

The sink or washbasin ought to be in the NE if feasible, since this is the corner reserved for water bodies of all kinds.

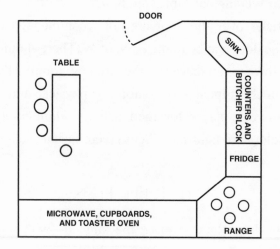

Figure 33. The kitchen.

The door of the kitchen should not be flush with any corner. Favored colors for the kitchen are yellow, light orange, or rose.

THE PUJA ROOM OR PLACE OF WORSHIP

Most houses in the Western world do not have a separate room for worship. This is a trend well worth changing. No matter what your religious practices, having a room of the house devoted to spiritual purposes can go far toward making a house feel special, and can have amazingly beneficial effects on your family life. NE, the direction of God, is the traditional corner for this room. Statues or icons should be placed on the E and W sides of the room. If lamps or incense are burned, they should be placed in front of the idol, but the materials themselves should be stored in the SE. Idols removed from temples, or antique idols no longer worshiped, are not auspicious. A little raised threshold at the entrance of the worship room is regarded as very auspicious.

If you cannot afford to set aside an entire room for worship, you can at least set aside the NE corner of whatever room does occupy the NE for this purpose. In India many kitchens have a little altar in their NE corner where the household deity is worshiped with daily offerings of food. Do not place your corner of worship in a bedroom, however. Another important warning is that there should be no toilets adjacent to this room.

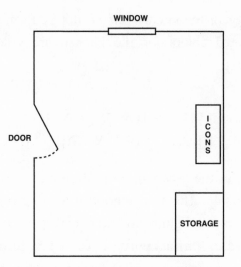

Figure 34. The room of worship.

Windows for this room are best situated in the N or E. Recommended colors are white, light yellow, or light blue. White marble is especially esteemed.

THE BEDROOMS

Master bedrooms should be placed in the SW, while children's rooms should occupy the NW. E side bedrooms are rare and are usually guest bedrooms. NE and SE are totally unsuitable locations.

Closets should be in the SW corner of the bedroom, while the dressing table ideally fits into the N or NE position. If you are habituated to working in the bedroom your desk can go in either the E or W, so long as you face E (the direction of knowledge and light). Place the TV in the SE, as usual.

Attach bathrooms and toilets to the W of the room. The bathroom door ought to be constructed from a single piece of wood, to ensure solid separation of the rooms.

Sleeping position is of extreme importance in vaastu. Ideally, sleep with your head to the W and your feet to the E. This ensures that upon waking your sight falls in the direction of the rising sun. Seeping the opposite way, facing W, leads to sluggishness. Sleeping with your feet to the N, the direction of God, is also acceptable, and is especially recommended for those following a spiritual or religious vocation. Sleeping with your feet pointing due S is permissible in the Hindu tradition only for corpses.

Figure 35. The bedroom.

Suggested colors for bedrooms are light pink, blue, or green.

THE STUDY OR LIBRARY

As mentioned, the W side is best for the study or meditation room. This allows one to face E, toward the open center of the house, while working. Bookshelves should be placed on the E and N sides but never in the NW or SW corners. Books in the NW corner are believed to be an inducement to theft, while books in the SW corner tend to be neglected. Windows should be placed in the E, W, or N. Toilets ought not to be attached to the study.

Recommended colors for the study are sky blue, cream or ivory, light green, or stark white.

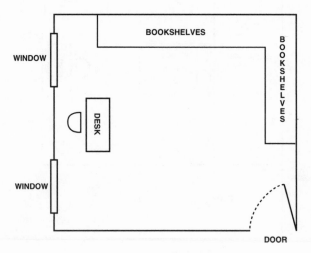

Figure 36. The study.

THE SAFE ROOM

Okay, so not many people have a separate safe room any-more—and those who do aren't telling!—but just in case you do, put it in the N. The god of wealth, Kubera, lives there. Vaastu does not recommend having the safe in the bedroom or the worship room. Wherever it is kept, the safe should have its back to the S wall and its door to the N, toward Kubera. This applies to any container that holds valuables. The SE and SW corners should be avoided. One inch between the wall and the safe is an optimum distance. Doors to this room should only be in the N or W, and it is desirable to have a threshold of 1 to 2 inches.

A safe should never be placed on the ground, but on a pedestal. Nothing heavy should be placed atop it. Within the safe valuables should be kept on the W or S sides.

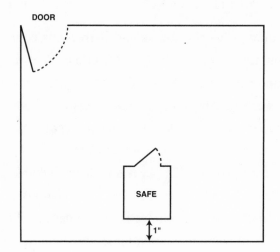

Figure 37. The safe room.

71

Cobwebs in the safe room—or around the house in general, for that matter—are an ill-regarded sign. They indicate a reluctance to work hard, relying, like the spider, on fate to provide. A clean house is supposed to be pleasing to both Kubera and his female counterpart, Lakshmi.

The ideal color for the safe room is light yellow.

TOOL ROOM

Lumber or waste should be kept in the SW sector. This section should be packed as tightly as possible. It adds to the "weight" of the house, helping to ground it. All tools and hardware should be kept in this sector. Dampness should be guarded against in this room.

BATHROOMS AND TOILETS

In the modern world, toilets and bathrooms come together so often that this is taken for granted. Vaastu, however, looks upon this practice as a disaster. When vaastu evolved toilets were usually in outhouses separate from the main building. It was universal in India to regard excretions as polluting, so much so that you had to take a bath every time you relieved yourself. This was a near unshakable taboo for two millennia, and even today there are bastions of tradition where this practice is followed. The unease an Indian feels on entering a worship room after having been to the toilet is hardwired into the collective unconscious. Modern India has devised compromises, such as vigorous scrubbings with soap and water, though the pious still go in for full-scale baths after every toilet trip.

Toilets are always sited to the NW, W, or SW, leaving the SE and SW alone. They are inconceivable in the NE or the center. The pot itself should be in the W, S, or NW of the toilet. The door should be positioned in the E or N. To read on the pot is regarded as a disgusting habit in vaastu thought.

Bathrooms without toilets can be in the ESE sector, with washbasin and shower in the NE, N, or E of the room. Tubs should be in the E, W, or NE of the room, in that order. Water outlets should never be in the SE or SW. Mirrors and doors are best placed in the E or N, but not the S. Always use light colors for the bathroom and avoid red and black.

THE FRONT DOOR

The placement of the main door depends on the owner's zodiac sign. Thus, if one's zodiac sign is:

Cancer, Scorpio, or Pisces, the door should face E.
Taurus, Virgo, or Capricorn, the door should face S.
Gemini, Libra, or Aquarius, the door should face W.
Aries, Leo, or Sagittarius, the door should face N.

However, may experts feel that since a house or structure may be used for many generations by many different people, the ideal position for the main door is difficult to determine on purely zodiacal grounds. A simpler rule is to take the square representing the plot and divide each side by 9 as shown in figure 38. Any door on the E should be in the sections marked 3 or 4. In the S a door should be placed at sections 4 or 6. For the N and W sides the door should be positioned at sections 4 or 5. Since front doors are usually placed in the direction of the driveway or main road, it may be more practical to use this method and ignore the zodiacal considerations.

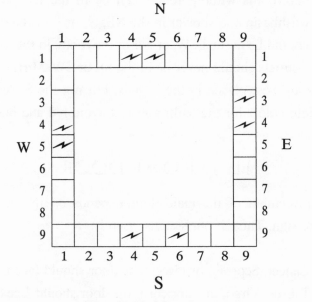

Figure 38. Ideal door placement.

THE GARAGE

No matter the type of building, a detached garage is best. The most favored areas within the vaastu grid are SE, NW, or SW, in that order. Under no circumstances should it be in the NE, but by now you should have guessed that. If the garage has a door directly connecting it with the main building, it is regarded as an extension of the building and throws off your rectangular shape.

MISCELLANEOUS TIPS

Three doors on one wall are a bad idea, especially if they are all facing the main road, as the house becomes too exposed to the road's energies.

Rooms on the S side should not have low ceilings.

Pillars and beams should always be even in number. Many a house in India has been demolished simply because it had an odd number of pillars. This seems overly drastic and modern vaastu practitioners have a more user-friendly solution: false pillars and beams. Sleeping or working under exposed beams brings ill fortune.

Circular staircases are to be avoided. The number of steps in a stairway should be odd and they should rise from E to W or from N to S. Steps on the E and N sides ought not to touch the wall of the building, though this is difficult to implement in practice. The usual solution is to make sure the steps are on the S and W sides.

Windows are especially recommended for the NW sector of the grid, the sector ruled by the deity of wind, Vayu. If the NW wind is allowed unobstructed access to the center of the building this is regarded as a sign of great good fortune. This is truly practical only in traditional freestanding houses with a central courtyard open to the sky.

Rooftops should slant from W to E and from S to N. Among other reasons, this was a defense against the monsoon rains of India, which come from the SW.

I will mention one other common Indian practice, though it has less to do with vaastu than with simple superstition. The "evil eye," a belief shared by so many cultures, is warded away in India by stringing together seven green chilies and a lime on a thread and hanging the concoction over your doorframe where everybody can see it. So pervasive is this belief that ready-made evil-eye–warder kits such as the above are sold at traffic junctions in metropolises such as Bombay. Personally I think the chilies and lime can be put to better use in your kitchen, but I mention it here because if you travel to India you are likely to encounter the practice.

6
INDUSTRIAL AND COMMERCIAL VAASTU

The ideal shape for an industrial site is a square or rectangle with a width/length ratio of 1:2. The SW and SE corners should be right angles.

The S and N boundary walls should be of thick stone (or concrete) if possible. The SW corner benefits greatly from the "weight" of a stone wall. As a rule of thumb the site should slope from the S to the N, and heavy machinery should be kept and used in the S. As the weight of machinery becomes lighter it can be allocated toward the N sector.

To build up open land in the NE sector is a mistake. Hills or mountains in the N or E are never well regarded in vaastu. Barbed wire should never be used around a site if it can be avoided; it indicates a fierce attitude that breeds resentment in others.

If the plot is divided into four equal parts, the main plant or structure, or the building having the most importance for the business, should be in the SW. As in residential houses, the center should be left as uncluttered and open to the sky as is feasible. A central courtyard where employees can gather and relax is a good idea for any business. The main entrance to the site ought to be in the E, N, NE, or NW. The S and SW are not auspicious. Entrance in the W is permissible if there is no other option.

As always, water bodies should be in the NE sector. This applies to wells, underground water tanks, fountains or pools created for their aesthetic effect, and aquariums. Wells or underground water tanks in the S or SW are not advisable. They increase the chances of accidents and brawls among workers. Water in the SE destroys productivity and causes worker dissatisfaction. Water treatment plants should be in the NW or W.

Furnaces, transformers, and boilers are to be kept strictly in the SE fire sector. If for some reason this is impossible, the S is a passable second choice. To put a boiler or transformer in the NE is a disaster.

As with a private home, storage rooms ought to be in the SW. Waste material can be stored there too, but there

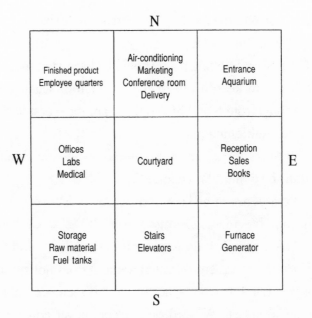

Figure 39. The commercial vaastu grid.

should be some "dead" space between the two. Finished goods should be stored in the NW. Generators go in the SE ideally, or in the E as a compromise.

Main offices, labs, and management offices are best kept in the W. In large plants, where workers live on-site, the ideal location for their quarters is the NW corner. If the quarters need to be expanded beyond the confines of the NW corner, or if you need the NW space to store the finished product, shift the whole shebang to the SW sector.

Medical facilities on site are best located in the SW or W. This is entirely different from the ideal locations for hospitals, because the needs of the two are different (see "Hospitals," later in this chapter).

The air-conditioning plant should be located in the N; one should strive to keep it out of the NE sector. Negative solar energies come from S and SE, so those are the worst locations for an air-conditioning plant.

Fuel tanks for diesel or gasoline or even coal should be located in the S and SW sectors.

Staircases are to be kept in the S, W, or SW sectors.

If your basement does not cover all the space beneath your building complex, try to place it in the NE, N, and E sectors. Since the basement is underground it does not get in the way of the desirable open space of the NE sector so valued in the vaastu tradition. A word of warning: never convert your basement into a garage, no matter how great the temptation.

The reception area should be in the NE or E, as these directions are conducive to relaxed frames of mind.

The marketing department should be in the NW sector and the employees therein should face NE. An office in the N with people facing E is fine too. An office in the W is acceptable, and the SW will do in a pinch, but not a lot of money will be generated. If at a loss, always have your employees face NE.

The conference room ought to be placed in the NW, N, or W. The nature of the room requires the mingling of diverse energies, so there is no ideal space or location that will eliminate conflict altogether from a conference room. All telephones are to be kept in this descending order of preference: SE, E, then N.

Research and development functions best kept in the W. The NW and SW sectors are fine too. The E and S sectors are passable for the short term, but they should not become permanent fixtures.

A sales counter is ideally placed in the N, E, or NE. The only caveat here is to make sure the sales person faces NW.

Delivery areas are best placed in the NW, N, or W.

Department stores should place their clothing sections in the E. The exception to this rule is women's clothing: the S is the direction for women, so items directed at them should be kept there, including clothing, jewelry, and cosmetics. Agricultural goods, seeds, and tools should be placed in the W. Car dealers should have their showrooms in the E or the WNW directions. Books, paper, or any other educational materials are to be kept in the E side of any complex. These rules apply to the layout of stores in a mall as well.

COMPUTER AND SOFTWARE INDUSTRIES

These industries present an interesting case. Because everything they do is involved with electronics, it is tempting to attempt to squeeze the whole business into the SE corner. Obviously, this is impractical, but computer manufacturers should at least have their core components manufactured and assembled in the SE sector. The office where key business decisions are made can be located in the ESE.

Unlike computer hardware manufacturers, the software

industry is involved with information and knowledge. Its key activities can thus be centered around the E section of the office or site.

In other respects the computer and software industry follows the regular precepts of industrial or commercial vaastu.

EDUCATIONAL INSTITUTIONS

The main roads ought to be in the E and W and the site itself should be a right-angled rectangle if possible. The main entrance should always be in the E or NE, never in the S. The reception desk should be in the S or SW sector of the main entrance. The largest buildings ought to be on the SW or S sectors of the site.

The principal ought to be placed in the SW corner, with the entrance to his office in the E or NE direction. The staff rooms can be in the NW, and bathrooms and toilets can go there, too. Toilets to the W are also acceptable.

Classrooms ought to be in the N or NE, with the blackboard on the E wall so that everybody faces E—the direction from which light and wisdom emanate. Libraries and labs should be in the W, but preferably on different floors. The library is "heavier" and should be on the lower level, if possible.

Administrative offices fit into the E or N sides. Playgrounds should also be to the E or N.

Dormitories can be safely sited in the SW or S, while

dining halls are placed in the W. Conference halls should always be placed in the N. Computer rooms go in the SE.

Favorable colors are white, cream, ivory, or light blue. Maroon can be used as an accent color for its energizing properties.

FINANCIAL INSTITUTIONS

A financial institution should be located in the E or N sectors of a site, with its main entrance in the E, NE, or N, in that order of preference. The manager can sit in the SE section, so long as he faces N toward Kubera, god of wealth. Reception areas will obviously be near the entrance.

Monetary transactions should be done in the N sector, with the employees facing E or N. Ideally such counters should be of polished wood, but do not round off the counter corners.

Other people in the office should ideally work on the W side. Safes should be in the S, facing N. If money is to be deposited, it should be received at a middle counter, not one at an end or a corner. Any money that is being given out as loans should be dealt with from the NE counter. Other payments can be made from the NW counter.

Records should be kept in the SW corner room, while regularly used stationery can be placed with profit in the NW.

As far as is compatible with acceptable taste, the walls should be light yellow in color. This is the color of Kubera.

FUEL STATIONS

Gasoline or diesel should be stored in tanks sited to the S or SW. Repairs and servicing should take place in the NE or E sectors. The manager's office ought to be in the SW or NW. Any canopy that is built should be in the SW or S, never in the NE or N.

It must be conceded that a fuel station is heavily dependent on the roads beside it and these suggestions may not always be practical. Yet those stations that avoid having the pumps smack in the central space do distinctively better than those that fill up the Brahmasthana.

HEALTH CLUBS

The swimming pool—no surprise—goes in the NE or N. Never put it in the SE or SW. The aerobics room can also be in the NE, but the E side is best. Machines are to be positioned in the SW or S of the hall.

The gymnasium, with its weights and heavy machines and exercise equipment, should always be in the SW. The S would be acceptable, but no other location will work. The steam room or sauna should be in the SE or S.

HOSPITALS

As much as possible hospitals should be built on the E section of a site, with the entrance in the E or NE. Admission and information desks should be in the SE.

Examining rooms ought to be in the N, and the doctors should face E when meeting patients. Patients should lie with heads to the S, W, or SW—not the N! Operating rooms should be in the W or SW, with the surgeon facing E or N. Emergency patients await surgery in the NW.

Recovery rooms should be in the S or NW. Toilets in these rooms should be in the S or W, with bathrooms in the E or N. (As we discussed in the previous chapter, vaastu prefers the separation of these two, though you are unlikely to encounter it these days.)

Equipment for examining patients, such as CAT scan machines, should be kept in the SE sector. Smaller equipment, such as stethoscopes, should be stored in the SE corner of the room where it is used. Medicine is best stored in the S or W.

The staff should have quarters/break rooms in the NW. This enables them to quickly attend to patients. Staff members should face N or E while working. Files and the like can be put in the SW. As with all other electronic equipment, computers go in the SE corner of a room. Accounts and administration work can be done in the NE section.

As always the central square should be left open for light and air, a practice many hospitals actually follow already. Preferable colors for the entire building are white, off-white, or light blue. Light green is becoming a favorite too and in many cases is ideal. Avoid pink, a depressing color.

HOTELS AND RESTAURANTS

A tank containing fish in the NE sector is good luck. The W is the best location for dinning halls, with the provision that people ought not to face S while dining.

As in private homes, kitchens ought to be in the SE. The walk-in freezer and refrigerator should be in the W of the kitchen; uncooked food should be placed in the SW. All ovens should be in the SE section of the kitchen.

Rooms in the hotel should have beds placed in such a way that guests' heads are always aligned to the S, with their faces looking E toward the new sun. Wardrobes ought to be in the SW. The dressing table should be flush with the SW wall, while the table at which the guest will sit should face NE.

Unlike other professions, the hotel industry deals with transients and hence the entrance lobby should be in the S or W—pretty dicey propositions in other contexts. Chairs for waiting guests should be aligned so that they face W. Staircases as always go in the SW or W, going toward the S or W. Storage should be in the traditional SW or S sectors.

The NE should be kept as uncluttered as is within the bounds of feasibility.

MULTISTORY BUILDINGS

A multistoried building is still subject to the other laws of vaastu—indeed it fits with all the other recommendations for industrial and commercial vaastu. Offices should begin on the second floor. (The exception to this is offices that are directly concerned with the administration or caretaking of the building itself; these can go on the ground floor.)

Elevators are ideally placed in the S or SW sectors. So, too, staircases, which should always make right turns for best results.

The main entrance for each unit (flat/apartment/office) should be, in descending order of preference: E, N, NE, W, NW, or S. Balconies are welcome on the E or N sides. Additional windows can be placed here too.

Penthouses should not cover the entire terrace but should occupy the S or SW sectors. This might not be always feasible, but always leave the NE sector relatively uncluttered.

As always the building walls ought to be higher on the S and W sides. The NE sector of the compound should not have large trees blocking it.

The security room ought to be next to the main entrance with a clear and wide reach of vision.

The recommendations in this chapter can help get your business off to the smoothest start possible. They should never be regarded, however, as a substitute for perseverance, tenacity, resolution, integrity, and the resilience that is so important for success in any form of business. Vaastu will work with you, but you must do your part.

7
AUSPICIOUS TIMES

In India, astrological calculations strongly influence life choices, right up to the present day. Vaastu is no exception. It is yoked tightly to the indigenous field of astrology, called *Jyotish vidya*, and the concept of auspicious times is key to deciding when to initiate various stages of the house construction process.

A great many of the ceremonies associated with the consecration of the house, site, or office are possible only if you have on hand a trained Brahmin priest who has mastered the necessary verses and the innate intricacies therein.

Ideally, the Vaastu Purusha is worshiped three times. During *Aadi,* foundation laying; *Madhya,* when the main door is fixed; and *Antya,* when the *grihapravesha,* or housewarming, takes place. Brahmin priests being a little hard to come by outside of India, I suggest you recite the following verse, from the Mayamatam, for your foundation ceremony—or better still, get your vaastu architect to do it. Whoever does it is supposed to recite while facing east or north.

I invoke the sacred formulae and the deities who reside within them. May they accept these words with grace. I praise Varuna, lord of all precious stones. I bow to the revealer of truth, Prajapati. May Lakshmi, goddess of wealth, be pleased. May Saraswati, goddess of learning, be pleased. May Vaivasvata, the sun, and Vajrapani, winner of the thunderbolt, accept my homage. I pay homage to the ever youthful Ganapati, the ruin of obstacles. May the glorious Vahni accept our homage.

A popular method of selecting plots or sites uses zodiac signs and numerology. Numerology is a system in which you determine which single-digit number is particularly auspicious for you. To do so, take each digit of the day of the month on which you were born and add it together. For example, if you were born on August 12, 1 + 2 = 3; 3 is your auspicious number. If the sum is still a two-digit number, add these two digits together: August 29 would be 2 + 9 = 11, then 1 + 1 = 2; 2 is the auspicious number.

You should look for lot numbers or street addresses that match your auspicious number. Again, these numbers should be reduced to single-digit numbers by adding them together: 24 Maple Street would be 2 + 4 =6 , while 196 Oak Lane would be 1 + 9 + 6 = 16, 1 + 6 = 7.

In addition to your personal auspicious number, each zodiac sign has certain numbers that are considered auspicious to it, as well as certain directions it favors. The correlations are as follows:

ARIES: N-facing site. Numbers 3 or 9

TAURUS: S-facing site. Number 6

GEMINI: W-facing site. Number 5

CANCER: E-facing site. Numbers 2 or 7

LEO: N-facing site. Numbers 1 or 4

VIRGO: S-facing site. Number 5

LIBRA: W-facing site. Number 6

SCORPIO: E-facing site. Number 9

SAGITTARIUS: N-facing site. Number 3

CAPRICORN: S-facing site. Number 8

AQUARIUS: W-facing site. Number 8

PICSES: E-facing site. Number 3

There is also a correlation between the number of the house or owner and the colors to be used. If the house number matches your personal number then it is an easy decision.

Number 1: light violet, pink, deep chocolate, red

Number 2: pink, white, all shades of blue

Number 3: white, green, ash gray

Number 4: pearl or ivory, white, yellow, saffron orange, sky blue

Number 5: pale gray, pink, white, indigo

Number 6: pale yellow, green, white

Number 7: pink, light green, white, lighter shades of blue

Number 8: violet, chocolate, red, pink, saffron yellow, saffron orange

Number 9: light yellow, violet, pink, red, orange

RITUAL POLLUTION

Construction activities are often delayed in India because of a typically Hindu problem called ritual pollution. This involves certain events that are considered inauspicious, and must be followed by a prescribed period of waiting until the energies are "clean." After a death no activities such as building a house can take place until the year of mourning is up, though the exigencies of modern life have seen this number cut down to a more workable forty days.

No construction can take place for forty days after the birth of a child, either. The birth of a child is not considered inauspicious, but forty days of respectful quiet are the rule. Indians, in fact, do not try to get anything done in the forty days following childbirth, an entirely sensible notion.

Likewise, if the wife of the homeowner is pregnant the foundation ceremony should be deferred.

And then there is the age-old horror of menstrual blood. All days of a wife's period are out to begin any construction activity or modification. This superstition is generally ignored even in India, though there are still pockets of vaastu traditionalists who adhere to it. Then there are vaastu moderates who point out that a woman's psychic energy levels are very high during her period, and this may result in particularly high states of tension rather than the calm mind that's ideal for what is inevitably a tense process anyway, so perhaps it is best to follow the old rule anyway. What one chooses to do is a matter of personal choice.

BEGINNING CONSTRUCTION

Construction of a house should begin only during these periods:

Phalgun (February 14 to March 13)
Vaishaka (April 14 to May 13)
Shravan (July 14 to August 13)

These dates are productive to the welfare of the family. The rest of the year is not well regarded at all. Many dire warnings are issued to dissuade people from beginning construction then.

Additionally, all construction ventures should be commenced only when the moon is waxing, not waning. The symbolism here is that during this time things are growing toward fullness and completion; after the full moon it's all downhill, so to speak. Days 2, 3, 5, 6, 7, 10, 11, and 13 of the waxing moon (in other words, days since the new moon), are considered especially fruitful.

Each day of the week also has certain qualities that impact the appropriateness of beginning construction then.

Monday begets happiness and prosperity if work is begun then.

Tuesday is inappropriate, and ill fortune will befall you.

Wednesday leads to material gains and joy.

Thursday ensures long life and happiness with children that make you proud.

Friday brings peace of mind and progress in one's work.

Saturday is popular in Rajasthan alone as a day to begin work.

Sunday, like Tuesday, is inappropriate, and ill fortune will befall you.

An additional point to keep in mind is that blue moon months—those with two full moons—are to be avoided as times in which to begin construction.

The grihapravesha, or entry into the new house has a similar set of auspicious times. A cardinal rule is that one should never have a housewarming, lock up the new house, then go back to the old house and slowly move in stages, as is convenient. Either begin inhabiting the new house immediately or defer the ceremony.

The grihapravesha is divided into three types: for new houses, for reentering your house after long travels or pilgrimages, and for entering your house after a major renovation.

The best months to move into a new house are:

Magh (January 14 to February 13)
Phalgun (February 14 to March 13)
Vaishaka (April 14 to May 13)
Jyeshtna (May 14 to June 13)

The month of Karthik (October 14 to November 13) can be resorted to if the need is pressing.

Tuesday, Saturday, and Sunday are ruled out as inappropriate times for entry into the new house. Days 1, 2, 3, 5, 7, 8, 10, 11, 13, and 15 of the waxing moon are beneficial. It is best to enter the house in daylight.

To move back into a renovated house a slightly different

set of rules applies. The appropriate months are expanded now in this order of preference:

Karthik (October 14 to November 13)
Shravan (14th July to 13th August)
Magh (January 14 to February 13)
Phalgun (February 14 to March 13)
Vaishaka (April 14 to May 13)
Jyeshtha (May 14 to June 13)

Sunday and Tuesday are to be avoided as days to enter the house. The dates of the waxing moon cycle remain the same.

HOUSEWARMING RITUALS

String up mango leaves on cords to enhance luck and guarantee the new house a prosperous life.

The elaborate calculations to work out auspicious times for entering the house are considered to become even more beneficent when family and friends are given a feast to begin the new life of the home in an atmosphere of goodwill and cheer. The traditional ritual is to boil milk and let it overflow and spill so that a comfortable, lived-in feeling is immediately established. This is also an act of symbolic magic, signifying the upsurge and overflow of one's good fortunes, and is deeply popular even with those people who have not the time or inclination to go through the long drawn-out rituals of tradition.

8
VAASTU AND
FENG SHUI—A
COMPARISON

Though India and China are geographically contiguous nations, they are two very different nations indeed. The crucial differences are environmental and cultural ones. Environment dictated geographical isolation and a historical ignorance about one another. The two systems of placement, vaastu and feng shui, share the same characteristics of divergence, as befits their countries of origin.

The most overwhelming difference between vaastu and feng shui, the one that seems to slam shut the door to any commonality of purpose, is the problem of the NE sector. In vaastu it is the most auspicious spot, one where you place your gods and wells. In feng shui, it is the gateway for devils, imps, and hobgoblins. How can two systems that purport to work with the same elemental forces of Earth have such opposing viewpoints? A little calm reflection will help us understand this divergence. China lies to the N of the Himalayas and winds can pour in from as far away as Siberia, with nothing to check their razorlike intensity. A NE wind carrying snow before it would indeed seem the favored entry for devils. India lies to the S of the Himalayas and a NE wind is a welcome cooling relief from the omnipresent heat. Snow is rarely factored into vaastu calculations, while feng shui has to keep it in mind. Stone constructions are possible only because of the lack of snow in India. Both arts are indeed being responsive to their environments, we just must keep in mind what different environments these are.

The ideal feng shui location looks like an armchair: a mountain to the N flanked by two armrests on either side, with a footrest hillock to the S. A little stream or rivulet should run past this hillock. This too is a choice guided by the geographical factors. The vaastu expert would prefer a stream to flow from W to E, ideally through the NE sector, and he would be rather apprehensive about the N side being the highest. Vaastu prefers the high-rising natural feature to be on the S as that is the direction of death and hence keeps injurious energies away. Also to the N are the Himalayas and any further buffers there would be superfluous.

As seen from this second example, too, culture and

environment all meld in a tangle that makes sense only on the ground it evolved from. Of course neither vaastu nor feng shui escaped the clutches of dogma, where directions auspicious or otherwise become fixed in mental concrete.

Feng shui literally means "wind and water"—that which can be felt but not seen, experienced in its long-term effects on people but not obvious at every moment as a tangible thing. Wind and water have the most impact on an environment.

The oldest extant definition of vaastu is *vasanti praminae yatra,* a place where living beings reside peacefully. Thus, in essentials the two sciences are in agreement about their roles—to harness the positive energy of the environment to benefit those living there. They are agreed in attempting to harmonize humans and their structures into the natural environment. Both sciences strive mightily to minimize problems and avoid generating negative energies and bad fortune, and wish to provide for happiness, good health, and comfort for people.

It can be instructive to realize just how many features these two systems have in common before some of their differences are delved into.

Both arts are adamant about having adequate knowledge of the history of the site being purchased. Suicides, ill health, poverty, bad energies, black magic—any place with such a history is to be avoided. Vaastu specifically mentions sites of those who were driven bankrupt or insane, and feng shui in principle agrees they are to be avoided.

Both vaastu and feng shui favor square or rectangular shapes. The *ba-gua* shape, the auspicious octagon, is also regarded as worthwhile by feng shui. The circle as a site shape is reasonably regarded in feng shui, whereas vaastu would never consider the circle because it represents the sky and you are then considered to be building on air!

The two systems are agreed upon the need for the land itself to be a bright green fertile area where abundant vegetation and healthy domestic animals can thrive: in China the pig, in India the cow.

As far as water is concerned, vaastu would like water bodies to be located to the N or E. Flowing water is welcome, but any pond, lake, or well is equally auspicious. Feng shui loves proximity to water; it is great good luck, especially if the house faces a river, lake, or sea. Feng shui prefers a gentle flow of water, however, a meandering motion that washes luck up to you, not a strong current that carries it away.

Both systems share a fondness for groundbreaking and housewarming ceremonies. Vaastu regards the *bhoomi puja* as mandatory while the *tun fu* ceremony is recommended by feng shui before the commencement of construction or before entering into possession of a new building.

In vaastu obstructions in front of the house—trees, open wells, pillars, posts, roads shaped like arrows—are to be scrupulously avoided. Feng shui too regards large columns and pillars in front of the main door as being oppressive of healthy chi, however a well-placed tree or statue can deflect "poison chi" coming toward your house.

Buildings at the far end of dead-end roads are a pet subject for dire warnings in both systems. Symbolically a dead-end road signifies that your hat is no longer in the ring of life. Vaastu warns that people will inevitably stagnate if they live at a dead-end and will gradually lose all they have managed to accumulate. Feng shui looks at a dead-end building as being practically a bull's-eye for the killer arrows of negative chi, which will chip away at your prosperity at an alarming rate. As a corollary, arrowlike roads pointed toward your home from any direction are bad news. If traffic flows away at a rapid pace however, then it cannot sweep away positive chi.

Plants and trees around the house are moderately welcome in vaastu, with the exception of horny and sap-exuding trees and plants. Feng shui regards trees as improving chi, but thorny or prickly plants are looked upon with horror: they provide too many bladelike points for negative chi to assault you.

Houses that are too close to public buildings are regarded as bad news in both systems. Movie theaters, factories, restaurants, and the like add to the pollution, the crowds, the noise, and the indiscriminate mixing of energies. Vaastu has a peculiar dread of being close to a temple, but if the temple is over a hundred yards away, then it is tolerable. The resident deities are supposed to be disapproving of anybody else flourishing beside them; the place should be dedicated wholly to the glory of God. Feng shui does not share this belief, but it agrees about public buildings, especially about the railway station's unsuitability as a neighborhood feature.

In India and in China, a well-embellished, impressive-looking main door added greatly to the prestige of the owner. Size, location, decoration, material—these are common considerations in both sciences. Doors that squeak and groan or scrape the ground or get stuck are bringers of bad luck for both vaastu and feng shui. The same belief holds for low ceilings, which do not allow energies to circulate freely and encourages the breeding of stagnant air. Fortunes are thus hampered. To sleep, or sit under, beams and rafters is singularly bad luck in both systems, it being, in feng shui's favorite phrase, "oppressive of chi."

Any projections of the building or site itself other than in the NE sector are regarded with distaste by vaastu. Feng shui considers all projections (usually) as unfortunate.

Vaastu and feng shui also agree that one shouldn't sit with one's back to a door. Medieval notions of alertness against danger do have a role here, but even in the modern office it keeps you from being startled or surprised, with the resultant disruption of smoothly flowing work energy. It's a good rule. Three doors in a straight line or row are considered as inducements for chi to whip through and take your good luck with it in feng shui. Yet in vaastu some temples have as many as thirty-two doors in one row, each leading to the sanctum in a straight line. This is considered auspicious.

The toilets and bathrooms present certain unique features. Even today old-school vaastu practitioners feel that you cannot really attain prosperity unless the toilet is far away from the house, or at the very least separate from the bathroom. The constraints of modern living make this impractical, so in an agreement of opinion, vaastu and feng shui recommend the lid of the toilet bowl should always be kept closed and the door of the bathroom shut. Toilets in the exact center of the house are open invitations to calamity in both systems, while vaastu believes in certain ill fortune if the toilet is in the NE corner. A bright light shining outside the toilet is a feng shui recommendation for keeping negative chi at bay. In any case the kitchen should not be placed opposite the bathroom or toilet. The same holds true for dining rooms in both systems.

Both vaastu and feng shui place much reliance upon astrology and auspicious times, though here it must be conceded that the similarity is very tenuous, the Indian and Chinese systems of astrology and methods of calculating auspicious times being widely different. India follows the zodiac, like the European system, but the Chinese allot specific animals to specific years, with much interplay of the dominant elements thereof.

This leads to one of the major conceptual differences between vaastu and feng shui. As mentioned before, the elements in vaastu are ether, air, fire, water, and earth. In feng shui they are earth, water, fire, wood, and metal and they are not elements as such but symbols of cosmic energy. Thus Chinese astrological calculations and feng shui solutions differ from the Indian systems, which emphasize the date, time, and place more than do feng shui. A person can be born in the year of the Dragon, for instance, but the Dragon can be Wood or Metal in composition and that affects the person's feng shui. The symbolic presence of an element has far stronger impact and importance in feng shui than in vaastu.

Where the directions of the compass are concerned vaastu is concerned with following the lines of force to build walls, but the real weight is given to the grid, as explained earlier. For feng shui followers each point of the compass is vital, having its own individual characteristic and power to impact some aspect of the owner's life. While India placed more importance in pleasing the gods within the grid, China was concerned with avoiding the unwelcome attentions of evil energies, ghosts, and demons. Vaastu has nothing like the feng shui geomancer's compass, the Luo Pan.

Feng shui possesses sacred animals unknown to vaastu mythology: the dragon, unicorn, and phoenix are concepts that just do not have any equivalents in Indian culture and hence do not affect any decisions. Indeed, other than the cow, and some stylized representations of deer and horses and cranes, vaastu is indifferent to animals, preferring to keep them at arm's length.

In the building of Buddhist pagodas feng shui showed its robust independence from alien notions of architecture. All across Southeast Asia the vaastu influence on stupas is manifest. But China took the philosophy and the relics of Buddhism and preferred its own architecture. Even the canons of sculpture are markedly different, bodily proportions being determined by varying aesthetic compulsions in the two countries. A fourteenth-century South Korean Buddha can still trace its roots to fifth-century Ajanta sculptures, but a Chinese Buddha is always Chinese.

Another variance is noticed in the fact that vaastu does not like armed or warlike figures, pictures, or portraits in or around the house. In contrast, feng shui uses such figures to frighten away bad energies.

The kitchen is important in both systems, but vaastu recommends that cooking be done facing E or N. In feng shui the position of the stove is a matter of precise siting, and an increase in burners is supposed to increase wealth. There is also great emphasis on the stove and the burner—the actual spot of the flame—being spotlessly clean. Many vaastu practitioners have now begun to recommend this feature as well.

In the matter of beds resting against a wall, the E and N sides are out of the question in vaastu. There is no equivalent of the ba-gua mirror to bring luck or even the simple feng shui expedient of doubling luck by hanging up a mirror at the appropriate spot. Vaastu also does not have a well-developed color theory to apply as rectification to problem sites, unlike feng shui.

A little-known aspect of both these arts could provide a fitting finale to this comparison of vaastu and feng shui. The beautiful peacock feather is viewed very differently by feng shui and vaastu. The Manchu emperors used to present them as a badge of honorable service and conspicuous success in some task. Placed in the S they bring fame, placed in the N success at work follows. In India, however, peacock feathers are regarded with extremely jaundiced eyes within a house. There are two reasons for this, one historical and the other mythological. Historically the Maurya dynasty (230 B.C.) were the first emperors of India and they wore this feather in the royal turban as a flamboyant assertion of their upstart arriviste status. (The first emperor, Chandragupta, had grown up in a peacock-breeding tribe.) The Brahmanical orthodoxy never could stomach the Mauryas; the dynasty was too prone to converting to Jainism or Buddhism and diverting state patronage to these rival faiths. They made sure that these upstart Mauryas got no posthumous memory in the history books, even calling the later Mauryas "demons." No token representation of the Mauryas could be acknowledged or tolerated, not even a feather.

In myth India's favorite god, Krishna, died because of his fondness for wearing peacock feathers in his helmet. Resting under a tree, he was obscured by a bush in front. A hunter released an arrow at what he thought was a bird displaying its feathered glory on the other side of the bush. Since then the peacock feather has been regarded as inauspicious.

9
QUICK
REFERENCE
GUIDE

This chapter is designed to serve as your handy reference notes, a quick guided tour through vaastu. Any time you need a brief summary of the absolutely vital points that must be kept under consideration at all times when evaluating or working with a site or structure, you can simply refer to this section. You could also photocopy it and carry it with you to a site.

MAGNETIC FORCES

Magnetic lines of force are to be respected and all structures should be aligned with them. This means that the E wall should be exactly oriented along the E line of the compass, and so on. Frequently however, a road or street is not parallel to magnetic forces, in which case the street becomes the new baseline to mark off the walls, which should run parallel or at right angles to it. In any case, the divergence permitted between magnetic direction and the natural orientation of the site should not exceed 12 degrees.

VEGETATION ON THE SITE

In these ecological times, this is an especially tricky issue. Any uprooting of trees should be done at least six months before the commencement of construction. After the structure is complete, ninety days should be allowed to pass before any vegetation is removed. In India, trees are precious and very often sacred. They are regarded as having personalities of their own, and may house spirits—personifications of the earth energies present on the site. Any uprooting is regarded as causing a psychic wound to the site, which may have adverse effects on the new inhabitants, hence the six-month recovery period. Once you have already settled into a site, however, your own dynamic energies are imprinted on the site and the removal of vegetation is not so fraught with negative consequences. In any event, vaastu believes in respect for the environment and the rule is not to clear-cut unnecessarily.

BEGINNING CONSTRUCTION

It is important to observe auspicious times when deciding what date to commence construction. Never begin construction during:

A period of mourning
The forty days after the birth of a child
Pregnancy
The wife's monthly period

MATERIAL

One rule applies. New structures need new construction materials, be they wood, metal, or stone. Recycling of material is acceptable only during renovations and repairs.

THE COMPOUND

Preferred positions for the compound gate are the NE, NW, or SW. Trees on the E and N sides should not be allowed to grow higher than the building proper, unlike trees on the W and S. This is a tropical climate precaution against the fierce afternoon sun. Pots and plants should be restricted to the W and S. Outhouses and sheds share this prohibition, too. Staircases should not be placed in the NE.

The compound wall or fence should always be irregular in height, with the N wall being the lowest. The W wall should always be higher than the N or E walls, while the S wall should be the highest of all. New additions or alterations are preferred on the S and W sides of the existing structure.

Storage tanks should not be in the NE (that's strictly for wells) or the NW. The SW is best for them. Fountains are always to be in the N or E.

HOUSE ORIENTATION

The main structure should ideally face E or NE but never SE. It should be square or rectangular. The corners of your house should not point toward any other house's doors or windows, as that sucks the energy from your house. Direct rays of the sun should strike the house for at least six hours every day. The contours of the building should not have any projections on the NW or SE.

ROOM LOCATION

The master bedroom should be in the SW if you are single but in the W or N for couples. The W is supposed to be ideal for conceiving children who will grow up intelligent and rich! A house should have an odd number of rooms. Any space with a door, including the washrooms, is to be considered a room for the count. Open areas to walk through should be left on the N and E sides of rooms. The space for worship should be in the NE. This is one of the most revered and insisted-upon rules of vaastu. The gods stay in the NE but the help are housed in the NW. The kitchen should be in the SE corner. The person cooking should face E, the direction of light and health. Sinks are placed in the NE of the kitchen, while provisions are racked upon the walls of the S and W.

DOORS AND WINDOWS

Doors should ideally be in the N, E, or NE of any room. The main entrance should not have more than two doors and should always open inward. Intersecting roads or trees before the main door are extremely undesirable. Steps at the entrance ought to be even in number. Doors and windows should also be even in number. Entrances should be in the W, E, or N, in ascending order of preference, but never in the S.

RULES OF HABITATION

It is not advisable to leave a house empty for more than 108 days at a stretch. The S section is the worst to be leased out and it should be kept occupied at all times by the owner. Rent out the N. The ground floor must always be inhabited, though upper stories may be left empty temporarily.

CONCLUSION

Having survived for so long, transforming itself along the way from temple and palace architecture to a more humble influence in individual houses, vaastu finds itself in a peculiar position in India today. It is popular, it is exceedingly influential, but it does not have status. It yearns to be recognized but answers all inconvenient queries from behind the shield of invoked tradition. The deep philosophical underpinnings of the art have been well nigh forgotten. There has been a revival, but no renaissance.

Southeast Asians always inquire of their Indian hosts

why the examination of their traditional systems is so haphazard. The answer is far too complex for quick or adequate replies. "Modernity" as an attitude is more socially acceptable among the decision makers of the country, and it is laudable to publicly profess such a belief. Any good word for tradition, any belief that it might be worth looking into, has to run a gauntlet of professed scorn and allegations of being backward-looking. On the other side of the coin, the inability to come to grips with a rapidly changing world leads to the embracing of anything traditional, and the rejection of all that is modern, by another segment of society. These two cultures share an abrasive relationship in the India of today. Otherwise sensible people, who would have normally given Vaastu a fair trial, fear being linked with the reactionary brigades that are on the loose in the country.

Architects are in a tiresome bind in India. After slaving for years to master their craft and produce appropriate designs, their hard work is overturned by a vaastu "expert" who may have no clue about modern architectural practice but has the superstitious ear of the client firmly in his power. Add to that volatile situation the fact that the architect is usually English-educated while the vaastu man may not have any facility with the tongue, and you have an "ignorant rustic versus culturally insensitive city slicker" face-off.

Vaastu has penetrated public consciousness far too deeply for the occasional outburst from maddened architects or hyper-rationalists to do it any real harm. The real danger is that it will stagnate at a dangerous level of half-knowledge.

CONCLUSION

There is no concerted effort to identify the ancient texts, res-
cue them from obscurity, and arrange for adequate transla-
tions. There is more jealously and petty-minded competition
than is good for anybody. And most tragic of all, there is no
consensus on adequate or appropriate standards.

In these circumstances, what powers vaastu is the
enthusiasm of the amateur and his or her standards of
integrity. You, the reader, having read this book, now join
those ranks of amateurs with the knowledge and openness to
apply the good sense of vaastu to your real-world architectural challenges. I am greatly encouraged by the fact that
vaastu is now gaining a following in the United States, for,
ironically, this can only strengthen its chances of maintaining
a traditional base in India.

Architects join this club in self-defense and may perhaps impose order on the near-chaos soon. Enforced famil-
iarity with vaastu has made a significant number of
architects realize that it is fundamentally sound, shorn of all
superstitious accretions. As a consequence, vaastu-compatible
houses and structures are now being worked out at the
design stage itself, rather than waiting for the break-it-down
school of thought to assert itself.

Having studied vaastu principles, architects can give
convincing arguments about energetically healthy structures;
they can prove to timorous clients that it is the spirit that
gives life to a structure, not following rules in a hidebound
manner.

In a very real sense, this is the most important development that has overtaken vaastu. There is an increasing recognition that the harmonious inner stability a house should provide is the true aim of vaastu, not the blind implementation of rules that may no longer be relevant. Vaastu seeks to enhance the body, mind, and spirit of the inhabitants of a structure, and that is a noble purpose. This book has sought to emulate that spirit—to approach the subject with humility, not blind belief; with reason, not superstition; with respect, not self-congratulatory skepticism.

In my still-evolving experience with vaastu, I feel its deepest lesson is that life can be lived abundantly. Vaastu is vibrance.

APPENDIX
COUNTRIES' VAASTU

It can be an interesting exercise to see how entire countries fare when placed against the vaastu grid of directions.

India, for instance, is quite inappropriate vaastu-wise, and a great many Indians state that to be the reason for its prevailing poverty. (This is nonsense, by the way. India was one of the richest nations in the world until 1757. British colonialism wrecked local industries, crowded traditional agriculture, and quite literally looted the country in a brazen manner that barbarians, Huns, Mongols, Visigoths, and Vandals could never match.) India's NE has no water body; the

Himalayas instead are placed in this sector. By vaastu crite-ria this is a large problem, and the perpetual strife in Kash-mir and tension with China would seem to bear this out. The SW and SE have large water bodies—open invitations to invasion. The E has shrunk, with Nepal, Burma, and Bangladesh going their independent ways. Overall, it is not a pretty picture, and one that is not likely to change, short of massive conquest and a herculean effort to fill in the Indian Ocean and complete the square.

Japan has more vaastu-friendly orientations, with an open eastern expanse and an extremely fortunate NE tilt to its upper landmass. The capital, too, is on the E, and the Pacific lying E of Tokyo should be beneficial. However, there is also a SW tilt to the lower landmass, and the SE corner looks snipped off. This would explain the ever present prob-lems of earthquakes and fires, the SE being the direction of fire.

The United States is exceptionally fortunate, its Great Lakes being close enough to the NE to bring luck and indeed actually connected to the sea in the NE sector. The W has mountains, another desirable feature. The country itself is an irregular rectangle and many state boundaries are neat rec-tangles or squares, ideal vaastu shapes. Even New York, which has flowing water to the E, and the right-angled grid structure beloved by vaastu, seems to be a vaastu dream come true. You can expect to see no end to this wealthiest country on Earth's continued good fortune.

RESOURCES

For a list of links to websites offering information on vaastu, including charts, background material, rectification solutions, software, and consultants, go to:

http://hinduism.about.com/religion/hinduism/msub-vaastu.htm